FEB 2 4 2015

D0460866

Kenya

Kenya

BY MICHAEL BURGAN

Enchantment of the World™
Second Series

CHILDREN'S PRESS®

An Imprint of Scholastic Inc.

New York   Toronto   London   Auckland   Sydney
Mexico City   New Delhi   Hong Kong
Danbury, Connecticut

Frontispiece: **Girls in Nairobi**

Consultant: Matthew Carotenuto, Associate Professor of History and Coordinator of the African Studies Program, St. Lawrence University, Canton, New York

Please note: All statistics are as up-to-date as possible at the time of publication.

Book production by The Design Lab

Library of Congress Cataloging-in-Publication Data
Burgan, Michael.
  Kenya / by Michael Burgan.
      pages cm. — (Enchantment of the world)
  Includes bibliographical references and index.
  Audience: Grades 4–6.
  ISBN 978-0-531-21254-7 (library binding)
  1. Kenya—Juvenile literature. I. Title.
  DT433.522.B88 2015
  967.62—dc23   2014031110

No part of this publication may be reproduced in whole or in part, or stored in a retrieval system, or transmitted in any form or by any means, electronic, mechanical, photocopying, recording, or otherwise, without written permission of the publisher. For information regarding permission, write to Scholastic Inc., 557 Broadway, New York, NY 10012.

© 2015 by Scholastic Inc.
All rights reserved. Published in 2015 by Children's Press, an imprint of Scholastic Inc.
Printed in the United States of America 113
SCHOLASTIC, CHILDREN'S PRESS, and associated logos are trademarks and/or registered trademarks of Scholastic Inc.

1 2 3 4 5 6 7 8 9 10 R 24 23 22 21 20 19 18 17 16 15

Zebras

Contents

Left to right: **Muslims praying, safari, Maasai teens, drying fish, Turkana girls**

CHAPTER 1

The Many Sides of Kenya

MAGINE A CITY WHERE BUSINESSPEOPLE RUSH THROUGH canyons of skyscrapers on their way to work. Imagine a city overflowing with people of all backgrounds, a city where you can shop at an upscale shopping mall or buy almost anything you need on the side of the road. It is a place where people can spend their days chatting in cafés and their evenings eating a meal of almost any cuisine from around the world. Imagine a city where after a long day's work, many people head to clubs to listen to hip-hop or African music. Then, imagine driving just outside the city, to a national park where giraffes, zebras, and rhinoceroses roam. In the distance, the towering office buildings are visible. You're in Nairobi, the capital of Kenya.

Opposite: **Pedestrians fill the streets in Nairobi, the center of business and culture in Kenya.**

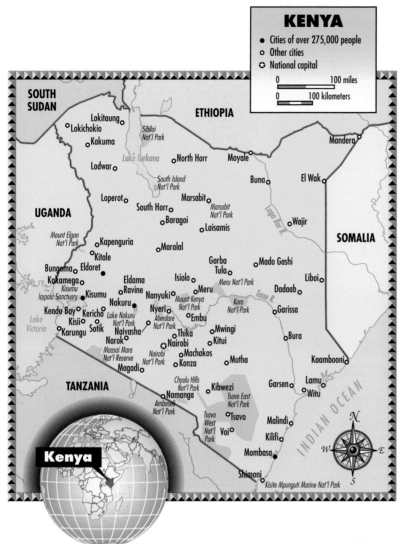

Many Cultures

Kenya is a nation in East Africa, where the warm waters of the Indian Ocean lap its shore. It is home to majestic wildlife and a wide range of landscapes. Kenya is also home to more than seventy different ethnic groups. Some of these groups settled in the region several thousand years ago. Others are more recent immigrants from neighboring African countries. Some Kenyans have ancestors who came from Arab lands and settled on the Indian coast. They helped shape a language and culture called Swahili. Smaller numbers of more recent settlers came from Europe and India.

Long before all these people came to the region that is now called Kenya, early ancestors of humans hunted animals and gathered food in the area. Remains of their bones have convinced scientists that humans first developed in East Africa. Because of this, Kenya and its neighbors are sometimes called the Cradle of Mankind.

Then and Now

The cultural history of modern Kenya dates back to early migrations of communities into the region about four thousand years ago. These early Kenyans raised goats and other animals and did some farming. Along the coast, East Africa was connected to the wider world through long-distance trade. In the 400s, traders from western Asia sailed down the coast. People from societies as far away as China used the Indian Ocean winds to sail to places like Lamu and Mombasa to do business. Europeans first came to East Africa later, during the late fifteenth century, but their influence was limited until the nineteenth century. The largest outside influence

Scientists uncover fossils of ancient humans at a site in central Kenya.

in the region came from Great Britain. Kenya was a British colony for almost eighty years.

The British built a railway that led to the development of the city of Nairobi, which is now Kenya's capital. The railway made it easier to bring goods and people from the interior of the country to the coast. The British forced native Kenyans off their lands so British settlers could start large farms called plantations. By the 1920s, Kenyans were calling for an end to British rule. They wanted to reclaim their lands, and their freedom.

Kenyans' long struggle against British rule finally paved the way for independence in 1963. Although Britain no longer ruled, English remained one of two official languages, along with Swahili.

A man on Lamu Island blows a traditional Siwa horn. Lamu is one of the oldest Swahili settlements.

Creating a healthy, independent Kenya was not easy. The country's many different ethnic groups did not always get along. For a time, just one political party controlled the government. Kenya's economy grew, though, as the nation welcomed businesses from other countries and promoted agriculture among its residents. Tourism now plays a major role in Kenya's economy. The country has preserved large parts of its land as national parks. There, wildlife can live safely, and both Kenyans and visitors can enjoy the nation's natural beauty.

Kenya, like any country, has challenges. Water is in short supply in some areas, and violence among ethnic groups has sometimes occurred. But the Kenyan people are committed to a free government and to building trade with other nations. Kenya has the strongest economy in East Africa, and Kenyans have embraced technology that connects them to the rest of the world. They work hard, but enjoy their free time, too, relaxing in the company of friends and family.

Tourists travel to Kenya from all over the world to see animals such as cheetahs in the wild.

CHAPTER 2

A Land of Contrasts

KENYA IS A LAND OF SO MANY DIFFERENT ENVIRON-
ments that it has been called "the world in one country." In
a single day in Kenya it's possible to go from an ice-covered
mountain peak to a desert to warm ocean waters. The nation is
home to rain forests, volcanoes, and vast lakes, as well as wide-
open grasslands where giraffes, elephants, and lions roam free.

Kenya covers 224,960 square miles (582,644 square kilometers), making it slightly smaller than the U.S. state of Texas.
Kenya shares a border with Somalia to the east, Ethiopia and
South Sudan to the north, Uganda to the west, and Tanzania
to the south. Kenya also has about 333 miles (536 km) of
coastline in the southeast, along the Indian Ocean.

Opposite: **A herd of camels in the Chalbi Desert, the driest part of Kenya.**

Coast and Desert

Kenya is divided into several distinct regions. Along the Indian Ocean is a narrow, flat coastal region. Tourists are attracted to its sandy beaches, and fishers sail their boats from ports. Mombasa, Kenya's second-largest city, is located at the southern end of the coast. Moving inland, the land starts to rise a bit. The Tana River cuts through the coastal region to empty into the Indian Ocean. Flowing for 440 miles (708 km), it is Kenya's longest river. At the northern end of the coastal region is a group of islands called the Lamu Archipelago. The major islands bear historic Swahili buildings and ruins, some of which date back more than a thousand years.

The Tana River rises near the Great Rift Valley, curves around Mount Kenya, and rushes through Meru National Park on its way to the Indian Ocean.

The Tana River also passes through a second region, the eastern plateau. A plateau is an area of raised, flat land. Great grasslands cover the plateau, but few trees grow there. Wildlife grazes on the grasses, and some people herd animals there, but farming is difficult because the land is too dry.

North of the coastal region is the northern plains. This is the driest region in Kenya, and plant life is sparse there. It includes the Chalbi Desert, near the border with Ethiopia. To the west of the desert is Lake Turkana, one of Kenya's largest lakes. The northern tip of this long, thin lake is in Ethiopia. Turkana is the world's largest permanent lake located in a desert. In the middle of Turkana are several islands. One them, Central Island, is an active volcano.

A woman fetches water from Lake Turkana. It is one of the world's saltiest lakes.

Kenya's Geographic Features

Area: 224,960 square miles (582,644 sq km)

Highest Elevation: Mount Kenya, 17,058 feet (5,199 m) above sea level

Lowest Elevation: Sea level along the Indian Ocean

Length of Coastline: 333 miles (536 km)

Longest River: Tana, 440 miles (708 km)

Highest Waterfall: Gura Falls (below), about 1,000 feet (300 m)

Average High Temperature: In Nairobi, 80°F (27°C) in March, 73°F (23°C) in August

Average Low Temperature: In Nairobi, 54°F (12°C) in March, 48°F (9°C) in August

Average Annual Precipitation: In Nairobi, 42 inches (107 cm)

Rainiest month: May, along the coast, average rainfall of 39 inches (99 cm)

Driest month: June, in the Chalbi Desert, average rainfall of 0.3 inches (0.8 cm)

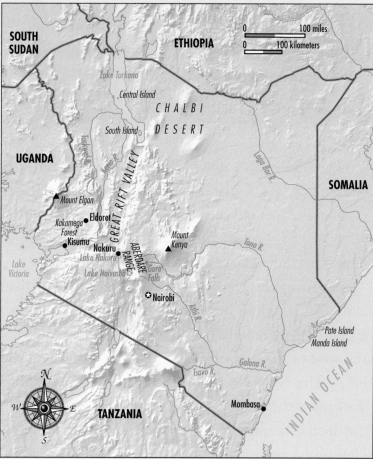

The Active Earth

A rift is a split or division in something. The Great Rift Valley is a split in the land. Earth's outer layer is made of giant pieces called tectonic plates, which are constantly moving in relation to one another. The Rift Valley was created over millions of years, as two plates slowly moved away from each other, a few millimeters per year. Millions of years from now, the plates will likely have moved so much that the land east of the Rift Valley is no longer connected to Africa.

The Rift Valley and Highlands

Lake Turkana lies at the northern end of Kenya's Great Rift Valley, also known as the Rift Valley, which stretches north to south all the way across the country. The valley is between 30 and 80 miles (50 and 130 km) wide. The floor of the valley sits as high as 6,200 feet (1,900 meters) in some spots, while sinking to about 2,000 feet (600 m) near the border with Tanzania. The Rift Valley contains a number of large, shallow lakes. The biggest, Lake Naivasha, lies in the south.

The Rift Valley runs through the center of Kenya's highlands region. The highlands receive more rain than other parts of the country, so they're well suited for farming. The highlands east and west of the Rift Valley have been called the country's breadbasket, because so much food is grown there.

The highlands feature many notable sites, including the jagged peaks of Mount Kenya, which soars to 17,058 feet (5,199 m). It is the country's highest peak and the second tallest in all of Africa. The Aberdare Range features lush forests and protects a variety of wildlife, including rhinoceroses, leopards,

The thick Kakamega Forest in southwestern Kenya supports a great diversity of life. More than 350 species of plants, 400 species of butterflies, and 300 species of birds live there.

and many kinds of monkeys. Gura Falls, the nation's highest waterfall, tumbles about 1,000 feet (300 m) through the forest.

In the southwestern part of the country lies the western plateau. This region includes Lake Victoria, Africa's largest lake. Only a small portion of Victoria lies in Kenya; most of it is in Tanzania and Uganda. Not far from the lake is Kakamega Forest, Kenya's only tropical rain forest. Also in the region, on the Ugandan border, is Mount Elgon, Kenya's second-highest mountain at 14,177 feet (4,321 m).

A Warm Land

The equator runs right through the heart of Kenya. The equator is an imaginary line that circles the globe halfway between the North and South Poles. People tend to think that the areas closest to the equator have warm weather. While most of Kenya does have a warm climate, there are variations. Much of this variation is based upon elevation. The higher the elevation, the cooler it is. Year-round, ice remains on the peak of Mount Kenya, which sits right on the equator.

Kenya does not have four distinct seasons. Summer and winter are not dramatically different from each other. Instead, the country is hot most of the year, with cooler temperatures at higher elevations. The Rift Valley and the highlands have a pleasant year-round temperature that averages 64 degrees Fahrenheit (18 degrees Celsius), though it can sometimes rise above 80°F (27°C).

The desert in the north has Kenya's hottest climate. Temperatures can easily reach 100°F (38°C), though night-time temperatures can fall to 70°F (21°C) or cooler. Areas of the grasslands in the southern part of the country also

Mount Kenya is a long-extinct volcano. It last erupted more than two million years ago.

Elephants cross a river in the Great Rift Valley during a rainstorm.

have temperatures that rise above 90°F (32°C) year-round. Temperatures along the coast average daily highs between 80°F (27°C) and 90°F (32°C). Helping to make things more comfortable are cool breezes that blow in off the ocean.

From March to June heavy rains fall across much of the country. Kenyans call these the "long rains." A period of "short rains" comes in November and December. January and February are among the driest months. Along the coast, the climate is humid, and heavy rains can lead to flooding. Mombasa often sees devastating floods.

In the desert regions of the north and east, rain can be scarce during most of the year, and some areas might not receive any rain for a year or more. That happened in the area around Lake Turkana in 2013 and 2014. The drought was so severe that some people moved to Uganda to find water. Other Kenyans who remained could find only roots and berries to eat or had to get food from the government.

Kenya's Major Cities

Nairobi, the capital of Kenya, is also its largest city, with an estimated population of 3,375,000 in 2009. Mombasa (right) is Kenya's second-largest city, home to about 1,200,000 people. Located on the Indian coast, Mombasa is an important port not only for Kenya but other East African nations, as goods arrive there from all over the world. The city is partially on an island, and bridges and a ferry link different parts to the mainland. Mombasa was most likely founded by traders around 900 CE. The Portuguese, the first Europeans to settle in Kenya, built Fort Jesus in the city, and it still stands today. The British took control of Mombasa in 1887, and for a time it was the capital of the British colony in the region. Many buildings in Old Town, which hugs the shore, date from when the British first arrived.

Kisumu (below), with a population of a little more than 400,000, is Kenya's third-largest city. Like Mombasa, it

is a port, but rather than being on the ocean, it is on the banks of Lake Victoria. It was built in 1901 as a station along Kenya's first major railway. At the time, it was called Port Florence. Kisumu has grown dramatically over the decades. In the late 1960s, it was home to only 32,000 people. Today, Kisumu is a center of trade and business for people living near Lake Victoria. Filling some streets are motorcycle taxis called boda bodas and three-wheeled vehicles called tuk tuks. The city has a bustling market that sells everything from food to furniture and clothing. Along the shores of Lake Victoria is the Kisumu Impala Sanctuary, a wildlife preserve that helps protect impalas, a type of antelope. Zebras and hippopotamuses also roam free over the park.

On the edge of the Rift Valley is Kenya's fourth-largest city, Nakuru, which has a population of about 300,000. Nakuru's name means "city of the waterbucks," referring to a type of antelope found in East Africa. Nakuru is growing quickly. Its location makes it a center for agricultural activity, providing support for the many farms in the surrounding region. Tourism is also important to the economy. Many tourists use the city as a base for visiting nearby Lake Nakuru National Park, which is home to more than five hundred different species of birds.

A Land of Contrasts **23**

CHAPTER 3

Wild World

HUNTERS FROM ALL OVER THE WORLD ONCE CAME to Kenya to go on a safari. *Safari* is a Swahili word meaning "journey." For the hunters, a safari was a chance to track down and shoot some of Africa's majestic animals. Hunting of big game is now illegal in Kenya, so safaris today feature travelers taking shots with cameras, not guns.

Opposite: **Giraffes are the tallest living land animal. Some grow 20 feet (6 m) tall.**

The Big Five—and More

Hunters on safaris once referred to Africa's "Big Five"—the five land mammals said to be the hardest to kill. Kenya is home to all five: the elephant, cape buffalo, rhinoceros, leopard, and lion. In 1977, Kenya banned hunting of the Big Five and all other creatures except for some birds. Today, the Big Five live in national parks and reserves across the country. Other animals that roam these parks include giraffes, zebras, hippopotamuses, antelopes, cheetahs, hyenas, and various kinds of monkeys.

The Problem of Poaching

Kenya ended the hunting of big game such as elephants and lions to ensure the animals were not completely wiped out. But elephants and rhinoceroses still face dangers from poaching, or illegal hunting. Many of the areas of Kenya where wildlife live are desperately poor, so some people who have no hope of finding a job turn to poaching.

Poachers often sneak into national parks and kill elephants for their ivory tusks and rhinoceroses for their horns. The poachers then sell the tusks and horns in other countries, where they are often used in traditional

medicine. In some countries, these prizes can fetch hundreds of thousands of dollars. In Vietnam, rhino horn is worth more than gold.

In 2014, the Kenya Wildlife Service (KWS) introduced two new methods to try to stop poaching. One is very high-tech: The group began flying remote-controlled drones over national parks. The drones send out radio signals, which help detect people who enter the park. The second method involves the KWS, along with officials in Tanzania, teaching students along their shared border about the need to protect wildlife. Kenyan officials want the students to explain to local villagers the dangers of poaching Kenya's wildlife.

Lions are the largest predators in Africa. Other African mammals are bigger, but they eat plants, not other animals. Lions hunt zebra, antelope, and buffalo. Another big cat, the cheetah, is the fastest land animal in the world. Over short distances, it can reach 70 miles per hour (110 kph).

Wildebeests are large antelopes with curved horns, striped necks, and dark, shaggy manes. Each year they take part in an amazing migration. About two million of them move together from southwestern Kenya into Tanzania and then back again. They make this migration to search for food and water. Other animals, such as zebras and gazelles, join them on their journey.

A cheetah chases down a Thomson's gazelle, its most common prey in Kenya.

Gerenuks eat the leaves off thorny trees such as acacia. Standing on their hind legs, they are able to reach the tender leaves and buds that other animals miss.

When people think of African mammals, they often think of the creatures that live on the plains, but other environments in Kenya also support abundant animal life. Camels are an important domestic animal in the dry regions of northern Kenya. Camels can be used to carry goods, but in Kenya they are used mostly to produce milk. One wild animal that lives in Kenya's desert regions is the gerenuk, an antelope with a long neck, small head, and large ears. Gerenuks stand on their rear legs to eat leaves off of trees. Anteaters like the drier climate, too. With their long, sticky tongues, they can lap up as many as fifty thousand termites in one night.

Many kinds of antelopes live in Kenya's mountains, as does the rock hyrax. This animal, which is about the size of a rabbit, is actually the closest living relative of the much, much larger elephant. A hyrax's feet have special cups on the bottom that help it cling to rocks.

Kenya's forests are home to leopards, which also live elsewhere across the country. Leopards drape themselves over tree limbs, and they'll even climb through trees to hunt for food. Other animals of the forest include bush babies, relatives of monkeys. Their large eyes help them see at night.

Mammals that live in Kenya's waters include otters, dolphins, and several kinds of whales. Five different dolphin species inhabit Kisite Mpunguti Marine National Park, along the southern coast.

In addition to good night vision, bush babies have excellent hearing. Their hearing is so good that they can hear insects flying and snatch them out of the air.

Reptiles and Amphibians

Many kinds of reptiles move through Kenya's waters and wilderness. Most are harmless, but some are dangerous. One of the most feared reptiles is the Nile crocodile, which can reach a length of 20 feet (6 m) and weigh more than 1,000 pounds (454 kilograms)! Tens of thousands of Nile crocodiles live on the islands of Lake Turkana and elsewhere around the country.

Other dangers lurking in Kenya's wilds include a variety of poisonous snakes. The list includes cobras, vipers, and Africa's largest poisonous snake, the black mamba, which can reach 12 feet (4 m) in length. Even larger, though not poisonous, is the

Nile crocodiles prey on antelopes, zebras, snakes, and many other creatures. Each year, they kill about two hundred people in Africa.

rock python. It kills by wrapping its 20-foot-long (6 m) body around its prey, squeezing it, and then swallowing it whole.

Africa's largest lizard, the monitor, also lives in Kenya. It can grow up to 3 feet (0.9 m) long. Smaller Kenyan lizards include chameleons and geckos. Geckos can frequently be seen scurrying through houses in the countryside.

Kenya also has a wide range of turtles. Tortoises are a group of turtle species that live exclusively on land. The leopard tortoise lives throughout much of eastern and southern Africa. It is one of the largest tortoises, sometimes measuring 2 feet (60 centimeters) long. Large sea turtles such as the leatherback lay their eggs on Kenya's beaches.

Kenya is home to about one hundred different species of frogs. The largest is the African bullfrog, which can weigh up to 2 pounds (0.9 kg). Much smaller and more colorful are the country's various tree frogs.

The monitor has a long, blue forked tongue. The monitor doesn't smell with its nose. Instead, it catches bits of moisture on the tips of its tongue and transfers them to the roof of its mouth, where it has an organ that can sense the smells in the moisture.

Quite a Crab!

Crawling along Kenya's beaches is the largest land crab in the world, the giant coconut crab. This shellfish can reach 3 feet (0.9 m) across and weigh 9 pounds (4 kg). The crab needs a long time to reach that gigantic size—about 120 years. Its name comes from its favorite food. The crab uses its huge claws to pull away the outer layer of the coconut. Then using a leg and its claws, it cracks open the coconut and removes the white flesh inside. The crab also tracks down and kills chickens and other small animals—including kittens. The coconut crab uses its sharp sense of smell to find its meal.

Sea and Lake Life

Kenya's lakes and coastal waters attract many fishers. Marlins and swordfish, with long, pointy snouts, are popular catches for visitors. Most are released back into the sea. Kenyan fishers, though, keep the big fish for food.

After men catch fish such as tilapia and perch in Lake Victoria, women lay it out to dry.

A row of red-knobbed starfish line a coral reef off the coast of Kenya.

Kenya's coast has miles of corals. Corals are relatives of jellyfish and other sea creatures. They live together in large groups, providing food and shelter for many kinds of fish, including brightly colored clown fish and parrot fish. Some types of coral have stony skeletons that build up to form a rocky structure called a reef. Coral rock was once so abundant that hundreds of years ago it was used to build many of the houses in coastal cities such as Mombasa and Lamu.

So many flamingos sometimes gather at Lake Nakuru that the water looks pink.

Wildlife Above

Rich in birdlife, Kenya is home to more than one thousand bird species, large and small. The world's largest bird, the ostrich, likes to sprint across southern grasslands or drier regions in the north. Ostriches can be 7 feet (2 m) tall and weigh more than 200 pounds (90 kg). Powerful eagles and vultures soar above the forests and grasslands. Storks, pelicans, cranes, and herons live along the water. The goliath heron can reach a height of 5 feet (1.5 m). Another waterbird, the flamingo, is bright pink. Up to two million flamingos sometimes gather at Lake Nakuru, in the Rift Valley, at the same time to feed on algae produced in the shallow lake.

The African gray parrot lives in the tropical rain forest. The fork-tailed drongo and the African paradise flycatcher are common in many parts of the country. Another common bird has a very uncommon look and name—the white-bellied go-away bird. On its head is a distinctive "hat" of feathers that stands straight up. And its name comes from its call, which sounds something like "go away."

Among the Flowers and the Trees

When many people around the world think of Kenya, they think of grasslands with scattered trees, a landscape known as the savanna. But along the coast, tall palm trees sway in the ocean breezes. In dry areas, baobab and acacia trees grow. The baobab stores water in its trunk which helps it survive dry periods. In the savanna, single umbrella thorn acacia trees sometimes stand out on the grassy plain. Their wide, broad tops look like an open umbrella. Kenyans sometimes use the long, thorned branches of the acacia to make fences for cattle. Tamarind trees also grow in drier areas, and their fruit provides food for some animals.

An acacia tree stands alone on the flat lands of southern Kenya.

Wildebeests cross the Tana River by the thousands during their annual migration.

Forests cover only a small part of Kenya—just under 7 percent. They range from the rain forest near Kakamega to forests found on the slopes of Mount Kenya. Some of Kenya's tallest forest trees are African mahoganies, which can reach a height of almost 150 feet (46 m). In the mountains, rosewoods and junipers grow. During colonial rule, the British introduced the eucalyptus tree, and it now grows throughout the highlands.

Closer to the ground, Kenya has a colorful range of flowers. The country is famous for its orchids. More than 250 kinds are native to the country. Many of them grow on the trunks of trees in the rain forest and other wet regions. In the savanna, firebird lilies produce red flowers that blossom after the rains. In lakes and ponds, freshwater lilies float on the water's surface. These and many other flowers brighten the varying landscape of Kenya. The region near Lake Naivasha has an ideal climate for many types of flowers, and large farms there now ship fresh flowers to Europe daily and provide jobs for thousands of Kenyans.

Protecting Nature

To help protect Kenya's diverse landscapes and the wildlife that lives there, the government has set up many parks and reserves. One of the most popular is the Maasai Mara National Reserve, in the southwest near the Tanzanian border. There, from July to October, visitors can watch the massive migration of millions of wildebeests and zebras. Elephants are a big draw at Amboseli National Park, farther east, while crocodiles and hippopotamuses are frequently seen at Tsavo National Park. Mount Kenya National Park protects the second-highest mountain in Africa. The park includes icy peaks, clear lakes, thick forests, and animals ranging from buffalo to colobus monkeys.

Most Kenyan national parks and reserves are on land, but some protect water ecosystems. For example, Kisite Mpunguti Marine National Park protects an area along the southern coast where visitors can explore coral reefs and watch dolphins leap and sea turtles dive.

The colobus monkey spends most of its life high in the trees, where it eats leaves and fruits.

CHAPTER 4

Creating Kenya

WHILE EARLY RELATIVES OF HUMANS WALKED the Rift Valley millions of years ago, the nation of Kenya is relatively new. For centuries, people hunted the lands, raised crops, tended cattle, and fished the waters but did not identify themselves as Kenyans. They belonged to different communities based on large extended families or hometowns. Some people identified themselves by the language they spoke or the religion they practiced, but Kenya as a nation was not created until British colonial rule in the late nineteenth century.

Opposite: **A scientist at the National Museum of Kenya holds a model of an ancient hominid skull from a skeleton called Turkana Boy. One of the most complete ancient skeletons ever found, Turkana Boy is about 1.8 million years old.**

Life Long Ago

Humans and their ancestors, earlier species that walked upright on two legs, are called hominids. More than two million years ago, hominids lived along the shores of Lakes Victoria and Turkana. In time, they began making simple tools out of stone and perhaps wood. These hominids may have been the world's first hunters. With some of the tools they made, they cut up antelope they had killed. They also used tools to chop wild plants that they found. Paleontologists, scientists who study the remains of animals and plants from the past, have found some of these ancient stone tools. They have also found the fossilized bones of some of the animals that were killed.

Over time, these early residents of what became Kenya changed. Their brains became bigger and they began to stand straighter. This process of change, or evolution, led to the humans of today, which scientists call *Homo sapiens*. Studying ancient fossils, scientists have concluded that modern humans first arose in East Africa.

As far back as two million years ago, hominids in what is now Kenya were using tools.

Important Discoveries

In 1965, American paleontologist Bryan Patterson uncovered an arm bone near Lake Turkana. After studying it, he concluded it belonged to an early ancestor of humans but could not tell much more. About thirty years later, British paleontologist Meave Leakey (left) found more fossils belonging to the same type of hominid. She was able to tell that it lived about four million years ago. Unlike later hominids, it did not hunt or have tools. Instead, it ate plants and nuts.

Leakey belongs to a family of paleontologists who have worked in Kenya and neighboring Tanzania. Her husband, Richard, and his parents, Mary and Louis Leakey, found many fossils of early humans in Kenya. The Leakey family has played a key role in uncovering the history of human evolution. Meave Leakey and her daughter, Louise, are still searching for fossils.

Into Kenya

About four thousand years ago, people who spoke Cushitic languages moved south from Ethiopia and settled around Lake Turkana. They were nomads—they moved from place to place following seasonal rains to find grasses for their animals to eat. Over time they moved farther south, seeking more water. People who spoke vastly different languages from the larger Bantu-language and Nilotic-language families also migrated into what is now Kenya.

These migrations were slow. Over hundreds of generations, small groups of Africans with diverse languages and customs populated the region. These groups brought new technologies and farming techniques into the region. They formed the cultural basis of the dozens of different languages spoken in Kenya today.

Kikuyu women perform a traditional dance. The Kikuyu people moved to the Mount Kenya region between the 1600s and the 1800s.

The groups that migrated into what is now Kenya had diverse lifestyles. The Kikuyu people moved into the area around Mount Kenya. They were primarily farmers, growing millet, peas, beans, sweet potatoes, and other crops. Because they lived in a mountainous region, they sometimes cut terraces into the hillsides to create flat farmland. The Luo people lived near Lake Victoria, where they fished, raised cattle, and farmed. Several different groups of Luo lived together, organized by clan, or large family group. There was no single leader, or chief.

Newcomers by Sea

Beginning nearly two thousand years ago, traders from as far away as the Arab-speaking lands of the Middle East sailed to Kenya's coast. Other traders came from as far away as Indonesia and China, in eastern Asia. The traders from around the

Indian Ocean reached Kenya on wooden sailing ships called dhows. Kenyans still build and sail dhows today. The foreign traders brought metal tools and weapons. The Kenyans traded gold from the interior of the region, ivory from elephant tusks, and other goods. This trade resulted in deep cultural impacts.

Some of the traders who came to what is now Kenya stayed, while some Kenyan sailors headed north and east across the Indian Ocean. Traders from other regions married Kenyan women and started families. Eventually, people from the Arabian Peninsula also brought the Islamic religion to the coast. For a time, the local traditional religions remained, but eventually more people incorporated their traditional beliefs into Islam.

Dhows have long, narrow bodies and large triangular sails.

By about 1000 CE, from this mixture of African and other Indian Ocean peoples arose the Swahili language and culture. This culture spread up and down the coast, from today's Somalia in the north to Mozambique in the south and across the island of Madagascar. Long before Europeans arrived in the region, these coastal societies saw themselves as part of a broader Indian Ocean world, where goods and ideas were exchanged across thousands of miles. Swahili communities grew wealthy from this trade and competed with one another for control of the most lucrative trade routes.

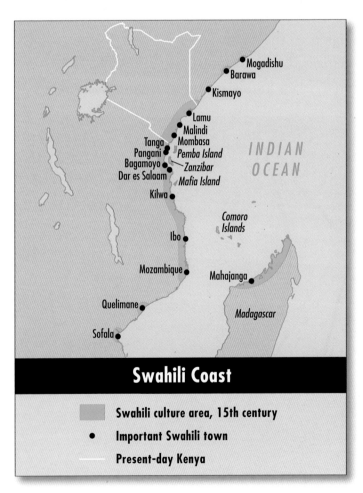

Swahili Coast

Swahili culture area, 15th century

• Important Swahili town

— Present-day Kenya

Europeans Arrive

In 1498, the Portuguese explorer Vasco da Gama landed in Mombasa after becoming the first European to sail around Africa's southern tip. The people of Mombasa did not welcome da Gama, as they wanted to protect their trade routes from outsiders looking to control them. But sailing north to Malindi, da Gama received a warmer reception. The ruler there was often at war with the more powerful city of Mombasa. He thought the Portuguese could help Malindi battle its rival.

Da Gama was impressed with the riches he saw in Malindi. The king wore satin clothing and sat on a bronze chair. Meanwhile, musicians played ivory horns that were as tall as they were. As a sign of friendship with Malindi, da Gama erected a pillar made of limestone. It still stands today. While in Malindi, da Gama also found a navigator who would help him reach his real destination, India. After he completed that voyage, Europeans began to trade with India by sea.

In 1505, a larger Portuguese fleet reached Mombasa, determined to attack and loot it. The Kenyans fired on the ship, but could not stop the European invaders, who killed many people and took all the gold and other valuables they could find. As the king of Mombasa later wrote, the Portuguese captain

Vasco da Gama met the king of Malindi in 1498. Da Gama led a fleet of four ships along the eastern coast of Africa and across the Indian Ocean to India.

"came to the town in such strength and was of such cruelty, that he spared neither man nor woman, old nor young, nay, not even the smallest child."

The Portuguese Years

The Portuguese continued to attack Swahili cities along the African coast, but their influence did not extend inland. By 1512, they had set up a headquarters in Malindi, and they later built a small church there. By around 1590, the Portuguese had gained full control of Mombasa, and in 1592 they began building Fort Jesus to guard the port. The Portuguese put a local

A view of Mombasa in 1572. The city had been founded in about 900.

Inside Fort Jesus

Few buildings from the Portuguese era remain in Mombasa. But it's not surprising that Fort Jesus still stands—the stone walls facing the sea are 10 feet (3 m) thick. Plans of the fort from the early seventeenth century show a number of buildings inside its wall. The fort itself has five bastions—locations in the walls that stick out, so defenders could fire in more than one direction at once. The fort is largely unchanged since it was built, even though it has endured attack and gone unused at different times. After the British took control of the region, they used Fort Jesus as a prison. Today, it is a museum.

Muslim ruler, called a sultan, in charge of the government, but in reality it was the Portuguese themselves who ruled the land between Mombasa and Malindi. The Portuguese also built another church and tried to convert the local people to Christianity. Most Muslims resisted, but some people who practiced traditional faiths did become Christians.

During the seventeenth century, the Portuguese settled farther inland and began to trade with the gold-producing regions to the south. Meanwhile, the Swahili along the East African coast began to challenge the Portuguese. In one incident, Muhammad Yusif bin Hassan of Mombasa led troops who killed Portuguese soldiers stationed at Fort Jesus.

The Portuguese sent more troops, but fighting continued when another foreign power became involved. Arabs from Oman, in the Middle East, sent sailors and soldiers to help the Swahili against the Portuguese. In 1696, the Omanis led a

Loyal to His City

Muhammad Yusif bin Hassan (?–1638) was the son of a sultan, or ruler, of Mombasa. His father was killed when he was a child, and he was raised as a Christian, given the name Dom Jeronimo Chingulia, and educated by Portuguese priests. He even visited Portugal and was received warmly by the king. After returning to Mombasa around 1626, he was made sultan. Still, he was insulted by a Portuguese officer. His father had endured something similar when he had ruled. The young sultan began following Islam again. In 1631, when he heard the Portuguese might remove him from power, he visited the Portuguese commander in Fort Jesus. He had his bodyguards kill the Portuguese commander and some of his men. The sultan's actions, some historians believe, were more about political power than religion. Like many Kenyans before and after him, he disliked being ruled by foreigners.

siege of Fort Jesus, surrounding it so no one could leave and no supplies could be brought in. After more than two and a half years, the Omanis and Swahilis took the fort. Portugal briefly recaptured Mombasa and Malindi, but they could not keep control. By 1729, they left the Kenyan coast for good.

Under Omani Rule

In 1806, Seyyid Said became the sultan of Oman. He ruled for fifty years and united much of the Swahili lands under his rule. Because of political instability in Oman, he even moved his capital to Zanzibar, an island off the Tanzania coast, in 1840. The sultan oversaw the slave trade in the area. People were captured inland and brought to the coast. Many enslaved people were sold overseas, but thousands remained on the East African coast. In Kenya, they served as household help or soldiers, but most raised crops.

By the mid-1800s, East Africa was drawing the attention of people in many different European nations. Some people came as missionaries—they wanted to convert Kenyans to Christianity. Others came to trade or to try to limit the selling of enslaved people.

The Path to British Rule

Great Britain had outlawed its own slave trade in 1807. It tried to end the slave trade in Africa, too. In 1840, the British opened a diplomatic office in Zanzibar. They wanted to make sure Seyyid Said followed the terms of a treaty he had earlier

Seyyid Said, the sultan of Oman, abolished the slave trade in 1845.

signed with the British government. The treaty said Zanzibar would no longer sell enslaved people to largely Christian nations, such as Great Britain. But British efforts did little to limit the lucrative slave trade in East Africa.

In about 1844, the first European missionary reached Kenya. Johann Krapf was a German Christian. He had almost no luck converting people, but he did translate part of the Bible into Swahili. He also wrote about Kenya, which led other European missionaries to go there. Over the next few decades, they converted more Kenyans to Christianity.

European explorers also came to East Africa, mapping the interior of the region. European nations eyed Africa's natural resources, which they wanted for their industries. They hoped to take those resources while selling goods to Africans. In

A Religious Explorer

As a child in Germany, Johann Krapf (1810–1881) knew that he eventually wanted to go to other lands and spread Christian beliefs. He arrived in Africa in 1837, heading first to Ethiopia. He settled in Kenya in about 1844. He learned Swahili and other local languages so he could speak to as many people as possible. Although Krapf was a missionary, many people in Europe thought of him as an explorer. He and his fellow missionary Johannes Rebmann were the first Europeans to reach the interior of Kenya, and Krapf was the first European to see Mount Kenya. The books he wrote about his journeys were popular in Europe and inspired other explorers to travel to East Africa.

1883, a Scottish explorer named Joseph Thomson mapped almost all of what became Kenya.

The next year, European leaders met in Berlin, Germany, to begin dividing up Africa. European nations claimed parts of the continent where they already had some influence. East Africa went to the British and the Germans. The Europeans were concerned primarily with how their nations might be enriched by the African lands. Some also wanted to bring Christianity and their ideas of "civilization" to Africa. Although many opposed slavery, they were deeply racist and did not consider African societies to be equal to their own. The Europeans had no concern for what Africans wanted. The boundaries they drew—which later became the boundaries between countries—sometimes put people from the same ethnic group in different lands.

During the Berlin Conference of 1884 to 1885, representatives of the major European nations laid claim to much of Africa.

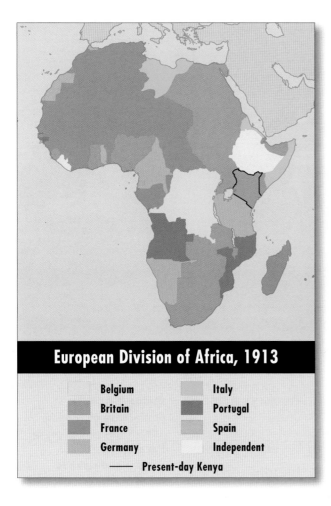

European Division of Africa, 1913

	Belgium		Italy
	Britain		Portugal
	France		Spain
	Germany		Independent
——	Present-day Kenya		

After the conference, Great Britain controlled most of Kenya and Uganda, while Germany took Tanzania. The British called their lands the East Africa Protectorate. It was also called British East Africa. A British company began helping white settlers come to the region. It also created a road from Mombasa to the interior, reaching what soon became Nairobi.

At first, the British mainly viewed Kenya as Uganda's outlet to the ocean. In 1895, the British began building a railway from the Kenyan coast into Uganda. Some Africans called the railway the Iron Snake. Some British called it the Lunatic Line. They thought it was crazy that the government would spend so much money on a train that seemed to run to the middle of nowhere. But the train helped open up the interior to British settlers who were soon encouraged to take land from Africans and set up farms in the highlands.

The Kenyans and the British

While some Kenyan communities reached peaceful agreements with the British, others fought foreign rule. During the 1890s and early 1900s, the Nandi, who lived in the western Rift Valley, resisted the British. So did the Giriama, who lived along the coast. To punish the Nandi for resisting the British takeover, British soldiers killed thousands of men and seized most of their livestock. They and other peoples lost their land to the British, as well as their political independence. Kenya officially became a colony under the control of the British. Local communities had to follow the laws created for them in Great Britain, rather than running their own affairs.

Kenyans also suffered in other ways. The British forced some to work on public projects, such as building roads and bridges. Any pay they received was low. Slavery was not abolished until 1907, and even then many Kenyans still lacked the freedom to work as they chose or earn a decent salary. The process of colonization, or becoming a colony, created a dual society in Kenya: The white British settlers controlled the government and the wealth, while the Kenyans supported the British by working for them.

To run the colony, the British appointed Kenyans to rule at the local level. This policy was called indirect rule, and Kenyan communities did not have the right to vote for their own representatives. Indirect rule further divided the Kenyans. Some benefited from British rule

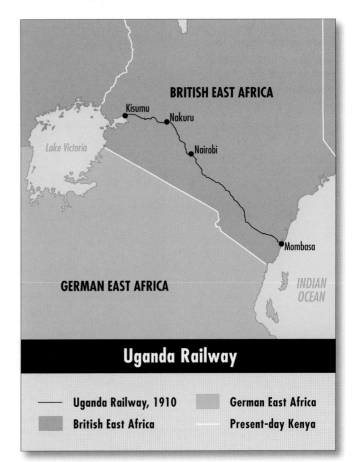

BRITISH EAST AFRICA

Kisumu
Nakuru
Lake Victoria
Nairobi
Mombasa
GERMAN EAST AFRICA
INDIAN OCEAN

Uganda Railway

—— Uganda Railway, 1910   German East Africa

British East Africa   —— Present-day Kenya

through this system, but the vast majority did not. Kenyans who allied with the British were often in conflict with Kenyans who opposed the British.

Two of the biggest problems Kenyans faced under colonial rule were paying taxes and losing access to land. Under British colonialism, Kenyans had to pay taxes but rarely received any benefit from this money in their own communities. The British also kicked thousands of Kenyans off their land and reserved millions of acres of the best farmland for whites only.

Europeans purchase ivory in Mombasa. The British sold whatever was considered valuable in Kenya.

In addition, after 1919, adult men were forced to carry identity and employment documents in a small box around their necks at all times. These identity documents were called *kipande*. Kenyans could be arrested for not carrying the kipande, and the information in them prevented people from being able to change jobs. They were one of the most detested aspects of British colonialism. Kenyans considered them a mark of slavery.

To protest British policies, some Kenyan workers formed an organization called the Young Kikuyu Association (many members of the Kikuyu ethnic group had resisted British rule). The association wanted the British to stop taking Kenyans' lands and create fairer tax laws. Other organizations pushed for better wages for workers as resistance against colonial poli-

Young Kenyans work on a farm belonging to a British settler. The British took much of the region's best farmland for themselves.

Kenya and the World Wars

As a British colony, Kenya was expected to help Great Britain when it went to war. During World War I (1914–1918), Great Britain and its allies battled Germany and its allies. Thousands of Kenyans saw action in a unit called the King's African Rifles. They fought all over the continent, including in German East Africa, which is now Tanzania. During World War II (1939–1945), when Great Britain and its allies once again fought Germany, British officials came to Kenyan towns and forced young men to fight for them. As part of the King's African Rifles, Kenyans took part in battles in North Africa and Asia. Black and white soldiers were equal on the battlefield, which helped dispel ideas of racial superiority. When Kenyan soldiers came home, many began to protest the racist policies of colonial rule.

cies grew throughout the 1920s and 1930s. The British largely ignored these calls for change, which continued through the 1940s. In 1944, a new national organization called the Kenya African Union formed to pursue the rights of all Kenyans.

Toward Independence

During the 1950s, the protests against the British became violent. The Kikuyu led members of other ethnic groups in a rebellion beginning in 1952. The rebels were called Mau Mau by the British, but they referred to themselves as the Kenya Land and Freedom Army. The rebels raided farms owned by white settlers and killed black Kenyans who supported the British. The British created a local army to battle the rebels, and thousands of rebels were captured and tortured. By 1956, more

Calling for United Action

Harry Thuku, a political activist, led the early efforts to oppose British rule in Kenya. He saw the value of uniting Kenya's diverse communities to work together against the British. He wrote, "What all of us wanted was to show people that we were all one family and that there was no [difference] between all the tribes of Kenya." As a teenager, Thuku worked for a while at a newspaper. That experience stirred his interest in political and social issues. He led the Young Kikuyu Association, which later changed its name to the East African Association. Thuku thought that Africans beyond Kenya should also work together to end colonial rule. In Kenya, he organized protests against the hated kipande system. In 1922, the British arrested Thuku. Thousands of his supporters took to the streets to protest his arrest, and twenty-one people died in fighting with the police. Thuku opposed the violence some Kenyans later used against British rule and eventually dropped out of the anticolonial movment.

than twenty thousand Mau Maus had been killed in the fighting, along with about two hundred whites and two thousand black Africans who supported the British. British treatment of the Mau Maus was so violent that in 2013, the British were forced to pay reparations to former Mau Mau fighters.

The Mau Mau rebellion convinced the British that they had to change their policies in Kenya. In 1956, they let Kenyans elect some representatives to the colonial government. Previously, all were chosen by the British. Even after more Kenyans were elected the following year, the number was still small, and Kenyans continued to demand more control over their own affairs. By 1960, the British realized they could not keep Kenya as a colony. Kenya would have to be ruled by Kenyans.

Kenya finally gained independence from Great Britain on December 12, 1963, with Jomo Kenyatta as prime minister. Kenyatta had led the Kenya African Union almost since its founding and had been imprisoned by the British during the Mau Mau uprising. The following year, Kenya became a republic, a form of government in which the power rests with

Jomo Kenyatta waves to a crowd in Nairobi on the day Kenya became independent.

The Father of Kenya

From the 1940s until his death in 1978, Jomo Kenyatta was a major figure in Kenyan politics. Born Kamau wa Ngengi, he later took on the name Jomo, which is Kikuyu for "burning spear." *Kenyatta* is a variation of Swahili words meaning "light of Kenya." British policies that took land from Kenyans sparked his interest in ending colonial rule. After working and studying in Great Britain, Kenyatta returned to Kenya and in 1947 became head of the Kenya African Union. When the Mau Mau rebellion broke out in 1952, he was arrested and spent nine years either in prison or restricted to living in certain areas. When he was released, Kenyatta resumed his place as a major political figure and attended talks that led to Kenyan independence. As president, Kenyatta tried to strengthen Kenya's economy. He promoted the idea of *harambee*, a Swahili word that means "let's work together." At times, though, he ruled almost like a king, ignoring the constitution. Still, his strong rule meant that Kenya remained politically stable throughout its early years of independence.

the people who elect representatives who are responsible to them. Kenyatta was elected president at that time and held the position until 1978, when he died.

Building a Nation

In the early years of Kenyan independence, the nation struggled to create a peaceful political process. Not all of Kenya's leaders agreed on the laws they wanted to pass. Instead of dealing peacefully with their differences, the ruling government treated opposing leaders harshly. For instance in 1969, Tom Mboya, a

Tom Mboya served as minister of justice and minister of economic planning and development before he was assassinated.

popular leader and early supporter of independence, was assassinated. He was a member of the Luo ethnic group. A political party associated with Luo and the political opposition was later banned, and some leaders disliked the way Kenyatta seemed to favor his own Kikuyu community over other Kenyans.

Despite the political unrest, Kenyatta's policies helped Kenya's economy grow. The government rebuilt a major highway and expanded the Nairobi airport. It also built schools and hospitals. Foreign businesses spent money in the country, and Kenya sent larger amounts of tea and coffee abroad. However, Kenyatta was unable to solve the land problem left over from the colonial era. By the end of his presidency, most of the people who had fought the British for access to land still did not have any land for their families.

More Recent Times

Kenyatta died in 1978 and his vice president, Daniel arap Moi, took over the government as the new president. Like Kenyatta, Moi held great power and he soon expanded it even more. In 1982, he outlawed all political parties but his own and limited free speech. When he ran for president in 1983, no one ran against him. Moi ruled for nearly twenty years more. By 1991, however, the political opposition had pressured the Kenyan government to allow other political parties to form. Though Moi won multiparty elections in 1992 and 1997, many people believe that he used violence and vote rigging to stay in power.

Kenyan president Daniel arap Moi greets the British queen Elizabeth II in Nairobi in 1983.

Events outside Kenya sometimes affected the country. In 1998, terrorists seeking to harm the United States bombed the U.S embassy in Nairobi. More than two hundred people were killed. Most were Kenyans. Four years later, bombs went off near Mombasa. Kenya also took in tens of thousands of people fleeing Somalia. These refugees were escaping drought and violence in their homeland.

In 2002, Mwai Kibaki became the first member of the political opposition to be elected president. Most Kenyans welcomed the change in government, and initially Kibaki passed a number of reforms that helped the economy grow. His government also began providing free education to all Kenyan

Rescue workers search through the wreckage following the bombing of the U.S. embassy in 1998. More than four thousand people were injured in the attack.

children through eighth grade. But Kibaki proved to be just as corrupt as the previous president. Adding to the problems was a drought in 2004 that led to a severe shortage of food. Drought continued to be a problem over the next decade.

Kenya faced another political crisis during the 2007 presidential election. Kibaki, a Kikuyu, was declared the winner over Raila Odinga, a Luo. But many believed the vote was rigged. Violence broke out across the country as people protested the results. About 1,500 people were killed, and nearly 600,000 people had to flee their homes. Kofi Annan, the former leader of the United Nations, helped negotiate a settlement. The two sides agreed to share power. Kibaki remained president, while Odinga took over the new position of prime minister. Kenyans approved a new constitution in 2010, with the hope that it would lead to a more democratic future.

In 2007, Kenyans took to the streets in protest following the presidential election.

CHAPTER 5

A Young Republic

ON APRIL 9, 2013, UHURU KENYATTA BECAME Kenya's fourth president. His name was familiar to Kenyans, as his father, Jomo Kenyatta, had been the country's first president. The younger Kenyatta took over a government created under Kenya's current constitution, which voters approved in 2010. A constitution outlines the form of a country's government and contains basic laws. The new constitution was designed to reduce corruption in the government, reduce discrimination against women, and give the people more political power.

Kenya is a republic. In a republican form of government, the power to rule rests with the citizens. They elect lawmakers and a head of state to run the government. Like other republics, the Kenyan government is divided into three distinct parts, or branches: executive, legislative, and judicial.

Opposite: **Kenyans celebrate the signing of a new constitution in 2010. This constitution reduced the power of the president.**

Uhuru Kenyatta casts his vote in the 2013 presidential election. Kenyatta won the election, becoming Kenya's fourth president.

The Executive Branch

The executive branch is responsible for carrying out a country's laws. Kenya's constitution calls this branch the National Executive, and it is made up of the president, the deputy president, and the heads of cabinet departments. These departments handle specific national issues, such as those related to education, health, foreign affairs, and the military.

The president is the head of the government and is also the commander in chief, which means he or she is in charge of the country's military. The president also handles Kenya's relations with foreign nations. The constitution notes that the president is "a symbol of national unity." Seeking that unity is important in Kenya, where in the past rival ethnic groups battled for power. To run for president, a person must be a Kenyan citizen from birth. The president serves a five-year term and can serve only two terms.

The deputy president acts as the main assistant to the president. If the president dies or leaves office, the deputy president serves as president until the next election.

The president chooses the heads of the cabinet departments, who are called secretaries. The president also chooses who will represent Kenya in other countries. The National Assembly must approve these choices. Also part of the executive branch, but separate from the cabinet, are the attorney general and the director of public prosecutions. The attorney general offers legal advice to the government, while the director recommends whether the government should investigate possible illegal activity.

Making Kenya Green

Kenyan women have had to struggle to make their voices heard in politics and government. One woman who succeeded in being heard was Wangari Maathai (1940–2011). Educated in the United States, Germany, and Kenya, Maathai spent decades trying to gain more rights for all women, not just those in Kenya. She also worked to conserve the environment and in 1976 started an effort to plant trees in Kenya. This became known as the Green Belt Movement. Maathai's group planted more than twenty million trees in Kenya, and the idea spread to other African nations. In 2002, she was elected to Kenya's parliament, and President Kibaki named her assistant minister for environment, natural resources and wildlife, giving her a chance to shape environmental policies for the whole country. In 2004, Maathai won the Nobel Peace Prize. The award honored her efforts to protect the environment and promote peace around the world.

The Legislative Branch

Kenya's legislative, or lawmaking, branch is divided into two bodies, the National Assembly and the Senate, which together make up the parliament. Members of both bodies are elected to five-year terms.

National Government of Kenya

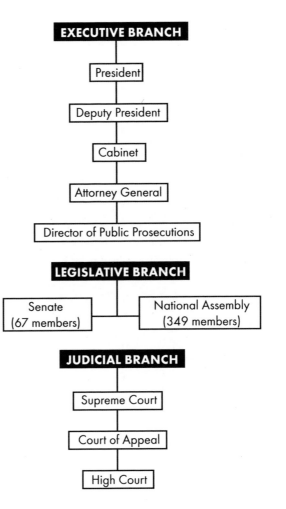

EXECUTIVE BRANCH
- President
- Deputy President
- Cabinet
- Attorney General
- Director of Public Prosecutions

LEGISLATIVE BRANCH
- Senate (67 members)
- National Assembly (349 members)

JUDICIAL BRANCH
- Supreme Court
- Court of Appeal
- High Court

The Kenyan National Assembly meets in Nairobi.

The National Assembly has 349 seats. Kenya is divided into 290 electoral districts called constituencies. One member of the National Assembly is elected from each of these constituencies. The assembly also has 47 seats reserved for women representatives, one from each of Kenya's 47 counties. The country's political parties choose the people who fill the remaining 12 seats, who are supposed to represent the interests of young Kenyans, people with disabilities, and workers.

The Kenyan Senate has sixty-seven seats. One member is elected from each of Kenya's counties. In addition, the political parties name sixteen female senators. Then two more senators represent the youth population, and another two represent people with disabilities. The Senate's main focus is on the counties, determining how the counties receive money from the national government.

Both houses of parliament must agree on a bill, or proposed law, before it is sent to the president, who can either sign it into law or reject it. When the two houses disagree on a bill, members from each form a committee to try to work out their differences. Only the National Assembly can sponsor bills dealing with taxes and spending.

The Judicial Branch

The judicial branch of government consists of the country's court system. Kenya's highest court, the Supreme Court, is made up of a chief justice, a deputy chief justice, and five other

Supreme Court judges hear testimony during a case in 2013. Kenya's Supreme Court was established in 2011.

The National Anthem

Kenya's national anthem is "Ee Mungu Nguvu Yetu" ("O God of All Creation"). On the eve of independence, an official commission made up of five musicians wrote a national anthem for the new nation. The lyrics were intended to unite the Kenyan people and express their highest hopes. The music was inspired by a traditional song from the Pokomo ethnic group. The anthem was adopted in 1963.

Swahili lyrics	English lyrics
Ee Mungu nguvu yetu	O God of all creation
Ilete baraka kwetu.	Bless this our land and nation.
Haki iwe ngao na mlinzi	Justice be our shield and defender
Natukae na undugu	May we dwell in unity
Amani na uhuru	Peace and liberty
Raha tupate na ustawi.	Plenty be found within our borders.
Amkeni ndugu zetu	Let one and all arise
Tufanye sote bidii	With hearts both strong and true.
Nasi tujitoe kwa nguvu	Service be our earnest endeavor,
Nchi yetu ya Kenya,	And our Homeland of Kenya
Tunayoipenda	Heritage of splendor,
Tuwe tayari kuilinda	Firm may we stand to defend.
Natujenge taifa letu	Let all with one accord
Ee, ndio wajibu wetu	In common bond united,
Kenya istahili heshima	Build this our nation together
Tuungane mikono	And the glory of Kenya
Pamoja kazini	The fruit of our labor
Kila siku tuwe na shukrani.	Fill every heart with thanksgiving.

The National Flag

Kenya adopted its flag when it gained independence in 1963. The flag includes three horizontal bands, black on the top, red in the middle, and green on the bottom, with white borders on either side of the red stripe. The black represents the African majority of Kenya, the red symbolizes the blood Kenyans lost as they fought for independence, and the green stands for the nation's natural wealth. The white bands stand for peace. In the middle of the flag is a shield like the one used by Maasai warriors. It covers two crossed swords, like the ones Kenyans once used for hunting and in battle.

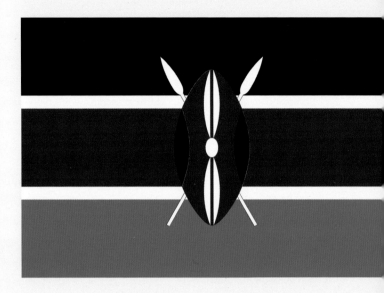

judges. Once named to sit on the court, judges can serve until they are 70 years old. The Supreme Court hears cases that have already been tried in lower courts, if they involve issues addressed in Kenya's constitution. The Supreme Court can also choose to hear cases if they involve issues of public importance.

Kenya's next highest court is the court of appeal. This court has at least twelve judges, but sometimes many more. In 2014, it had twenty-six. The court handles appeals, or requests to hear the facts of a case already decided in a lower court. These cases usually come from the high court, which handles cases regarding crimes or disputes between citizens. The high court also hears cases that affect rights or freedoms spelled out in the bill of rights, which was introduced with the 2010 constitution. The United States has a bill of rights spelling out political rights and freedoms. Kenya's, though, also guarantees such things as access to food, housing, and water.

Kenya also has some other courts that deal with minor disputes or specialized cases. For example, cases involving issues such as divorce and inheritance can be heard in Kadhis' courts, which apply Islamic law, if all the people involved agree to it.

County and Local Government

Kenya is divided into forty-seven counties. Each has a county assembly that makes local laws, and a county executive, called a governor, who carries them out. Like the president,

A lawyer in Nairobi presents evidence in a case involving a man caught smuggling ivory.

Kenya's Capital

The coming of the railway to Kenya led to Nairobi being founded in 1899 as a supply depot. Its name comes from a Maasai expression that means "place of cold water." Maasai herders once brought their cattle to the area to drink. The British made Nairobi the capital of the East African Protectorate, in part because the climate was cooler there than along the coast. Nairobi's elevation of about 5,500 feet (1,680 m) helps keep the temperature down, with average highs between 73°F and 80°F (23°C and 27°C) throughout the year.

Nairobi is the center of Kenya's economic life as well as its government. Many industries are located in and around the city, and crops grown in the highlands often pass through Nairobi before they're shipped overseas. Nairobi is also the financial center for all of East Africa. Its downtown is filled with skyscrapers. The

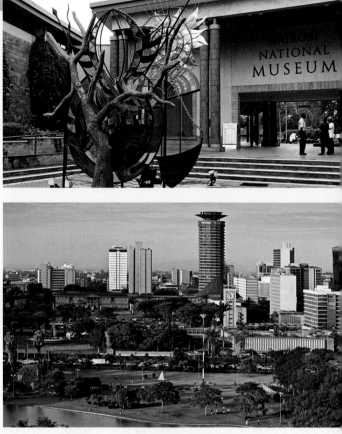

hope of finding jobs draws people from the countryside. Nairobi's estimated population in 2009 was more than 3.3 million. Many of the residents are poor and live in crowded conditions.

Visitors to Nairobi enjoy the City Market in the center of the city, which sells local foods and goods from all over Africa. Kenya's history comes to life at the Nairobi National Museum. Just outside the city is Nairobi National Park, where zebras, giraffes, and other animals roam.

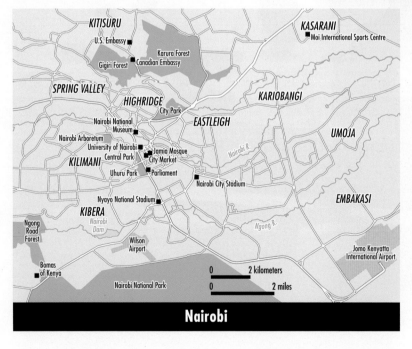

Nairobi

the governor picks the heads of different departments, such as transportation, education, and agriculture. County governments also handle health care, fight fires, provide clean water, and enforce national laws regarding the environment.

In cities and towns, Kenyans elect members to a governing body called a council. Larger communities have mayors and deputy mayors in addition to councils. Each council meets at least four times a year to conduct its business. The local governments address such issues as keeping records, improving roads, and promoting good health.

Workers construct a road in northern Kenya. Both the national and local governments are involved in road construction.

CHAPTER 6

Making a Living

A WALK THROUGH DOWNTOWN NAIROBI REVEALS a bustling, modern city with business ties to the rest of the world. Far from the capital, many Kenyans still herd cattle or farm as their main profession. Kenyans make their livings in many different ways. But for many people in Kenya, finding a job is a challenge—one the government hopes to fix by growing the economy as a whole.

Opposite: **Workers spread coffee beans to dry. Kenya produces more than 110 million pounds (50 million kg) of coffee every year.**

Producing Food

Kenya's economy relies heavily on the crops and animals its farmers raise. About 75 percent of Kenyans work in agriculture. Most farmers own only small plots of land, though large coffee and tea plantations established during colonial days still exist. Crops grow in a limited area—about 20 percent of the country—where the rainfall is highest, such as in the Rift Valley, the highlands, and near the coast. Except during droughts, the country's farmers can produce enough food for everyone in Kenya. Some of the crops grown include corn, bananas, wheat, and sugarcane.

From Bananas to Baked Goods

Kenyans eat a lot of bananas, and most of them come from local farmers. The farmers, however, have often struggled to get their fruit to the market before it rots. When the harvest comes, there are more bananas available than people want to buy. Eric Muthomi figured out a way to help banana farmers in his native region of Meru, in central Kenya. In 2011, Muthomi started a company called Stawi Foods and Fruit. The company promised banana farmers a fair price for all the fruit they could grow. Instead of storing the fruit, Muthomi turned it into a healthy banana flour that Kenyans could use to make baby food, porridge, and baked goods. As the company grew, it introduced several other products, one of which uses grains grown in Kenya. Muthomi is both running a successful business and helping local farmers. He says, "I am happy when farmers come up to me and thank me for getting them a market for their product. It is such a satisfying feeling."

Many Kenyan farmers raise crops they can export, or sell abroad. Tea and coffee top the list, though the country also exports fruits, vegetables, and flowers. Agricultural products as a whole are Kenya's leading exports, which totaled just over US$6 billion in 2012. Overall, most exports go to Uganda, Tanzania, European countries, and the United States.

Kenyans raise pigs and chickens. They also keep cows, goats, and camels for their milk.

Fishing is important in the coastal and lake regions. Tuna and shark are caught along the coast, as are shellfish, octopus, and squid. In Lake Victoria and other freshwater lakes, fishers catch tilapia and Nile perch. Kenya is also increasing produc-

Men bring their fishing catch ashore at Malindi. Major catch include sailfish, kingfish, tuna, and marlin.

tion in its aquaculture industry, which is the raising of fish for food. Tilapia and catfish are being grown in freshly dug ponds around the country.

From the Earth

Kenya has a small but growing mining industry. Mining companies typically unearth industrial minerals that are used to make such products as glass, chemicals, and metals. These minerals include soda ash, raw crushed soda, fluorspar, lime,

An engineer walks past an oil rig in the Lake Turkana region.

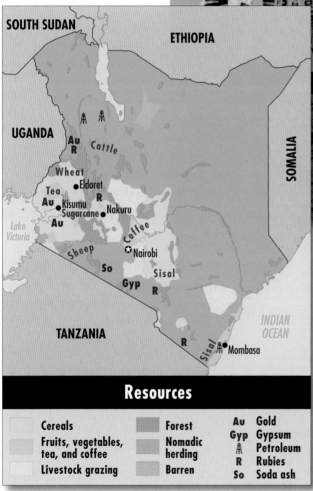

Resources

Cereals	Forest	Au	Gold
Fruits, vegetables, tea, and coffee	Nomadic herding	Gyp	Gypsum
Livestock grazing	Barren	R	Petroleum
		So	Rubies
			Soda ash

salt, and gypsum. The country does mine some gold and gems, including rubies and topazes.

Another important resource is petroleum, or oil, which was discovered in northern Kenya, between Lake Turkana and Uganda, in 2012. Experts predict the country could make $10 billion over 30 years selling the oil overseas. Uganda and Kenya

Seeking the Sun

Like most of the world, Kenya burns oil to generate some of its electricity. Burning oil, however, sends pollutants into the air, harming the environment. Kenya gets just over 40 percent of its electricity from rivers that power the generation plants. Geothermal energy (top left), electricity produced by using the heat inside the earth, accounts for another 20 percent of Kenya's electricity. It is especially important in the Rift Valley.

In recent years, the nation has also been turning to the sun for power. In 2010, women in rural villages near Kisumu began using solar power (bottom left) for their electrical needs. As a result, they don't have to burn as much wood for light or for cooking. Burning wood, like burning oil, causes pollution. Using the sun to produce electricity also helps the women economically. The solar energy powers a small mill, giving the women a chance to start their own business and earn money. In 2014, the Kenyan government announced it would build nine large solar power plants across the country, making electricity cheaper and reducing pollution.

are working together to build a pipeline to pump the oil to the Kenyan coast. To go along with this pipeline, a new port is being built in the coastal town of Lamu. It will help Kenya as well as neighboring countries such as Ethiopia, Uganda, and South Sudan import and export their goods.

Making Goods

Kenyans manufacture a wide range of goods. The largest part of the manufacturing sector involves processing food and

What Kenya Grows, Makes, and Mines

AGRICULTURE (2012)

Sugarcane	5,822,633 metric tons
Corn	3,600,000 metric tons
Bananas	1,197,988 metric tons

MANUFACTURING (VALUE, 2010)

Food products	US$607,000,000
Glass products	US$562,000,000
Beverages	US$281,000,9991

MINING (2011)

Soda ash	499,100 metric tons
Fluorspar	117,420 metric tons
Rubies	5,500 kilograms

drinks. The nation also produces cars, plastic goods, clothing, chemicals and medicines, paper and paper products, and electrical equipment. Most of the goods are sold within Kenya.

Serving Others

The largest part of Kenya's economy is the service sector. This part of the economy includes banking, education, health care, selling goods, and selling property.

A large part of the service sector in Kenya is devoted to tourism. Over one million visitors arrive in Kenya each year, and they spend more than one billion dollars. The tourism industry employs people in hotels and restaurants and as guides on safaris.

The service sector also includes what is called the informal economy. In Nairobi in particular, many street vendors do not register their businesses with the government. They sell everything from clothes to DVDs to food on the street, without paying rent or taxes. Other members of the informal

A man displays sandals made from old tires. These sandals last about ten times longer than traditional shoes.

Kenyan Currency

Kenya's basic unit of money is the Kenyan shilling. One shilling is divided into 100 cents. Paper money comes in bills worth 50, 100, 200, 500, and 1,000 Kenyan shillings. All have an image of Jomo Kenyatta on the front. On the back are different scenes of life in Kenya, such as elephants grazing and cotton being harvested. Coins come in values of 50 cents, and 1, 5, 10, 20, and 40 Kenyan shillings. All except the 40-shilling piece depict Kenyatta on the front. The 20-shilling coin features Kenya's third president, Mwai Kibaki. In 2014, 88 Kenyan shillings equaled US$1.

economy perform services such as carpentry or shoe shining. Still others make goods for Kenyans to buy. Some people, for example, make sandals out of old tires from vehicles.

The Chinese government is helping build roads and railroads in Kenya, so China can move goods through the country more easily.

Many young people work in the informal economy because they can't find other work. The unemployment rate—the percentage of working-age people who cannot find jobs—is estimated at more than 30 percent.

Money from foreign sources is helping Kenya improve its economy. China, for example, is spending billions of dollars to rebuild the railroad from Mombasa to Uganda and to develop better roads to link Kenya with Ethiopia. This will help China gain access to Kenya's raw materials and markets. Money also flows into the country from Kenyans working abroad. They send nearly a billion dollars home to their relatives each year.

Keeping Connected

Kenya is a leader in East Africa in communications. Although there are few landlines in the country, most Kenyans have cell phones. Safaricom, the nation's leading cell service provider, is one of the nation's most successful businesses. Internet usage is also growing by leaps and bounds in Kenya. In 2010, only about 10 percent of Kenyans used the Internet. By 2013, 39 percent were Internet users.

Many Kenyans use their cell phones to do banking. M-Pesa, the world's leading mobile money system, is used by two-thirds of the adults in Kenya. Using M-Pesa, Kenyans can deposit paychecks and withdraw cash. They can pay the rent, buy groceries, and transfer money to anyone else with an M-Pesa account, all without ever having to go to the bank.

CHAPTER 7

Diverse People

A PERSON TRAVELING ACROSS KENYA WILL HEAR many different languages. Almost everyone speaks Swahili, one of Kenya's two official languages. In Nairobi and other cities, many people speak English, the other official language. In rural areas, people speak various languages. All together, Kenyans speak about sixty different languages, and most people speak at least three. The variety of languages reflects the many ethnic groups that make up the nation.

Opposite: **Children make up the largest age group in Kenya. About 42 percent of the population is younger than fifteen years old.**

The Common Language

Many languages spoken in Kenya belong to the Bantu language family, which includes about five hundred languages spoken in various parts of Africa. Swahili is one of them. It is a coastal trading language that reflects the interconnected nature of societies that bordered the Indian Ocean many centuries ago. Though 85 percent of the words in Swahili have African ori-

Common Swahili Words

jambo	hello
kwaheri	good-bye
ndiyo	yes
hapana	no
tafadhali	please
asante	thank you

gins, 15 percent come from other languages, including Arabic, Portuguese, and Hindi, a language spoken in India. Today, 100 million people speak Swahili in East Africa, but for most it is not their first language. Swahili is probably the most common African language now broadcast on world radio stations and taught in international universities.

Many signs in Kenya are written in both English and Swahili.

Old and Young

Kenya is a mostly rural country—only about 25 percent of the population lives in cities and the surrounding areas. Most people live in the central and western regions of the country

Some rural homes have roofs made of grasses.

Swahili in English

The English language borrows words and phrases from all over the world, including the Swahili spoken in Kenya. The movie *The Lion King* used the phrase *hakuna matata*, which is Swahili for "no problem." And the name of the star lion, Simba (left), is the Swahili word for "lion." Fans of *Star Trek* know the character named Uhuru, which is Swahili for "freedom." *Safari* is another Swahili word, as is *Kwanzaa*, the name of a holiday some African Americans celebrate at the end of December. The name comes from the phrase *matunda ya kwanza*, which means "first fruits."

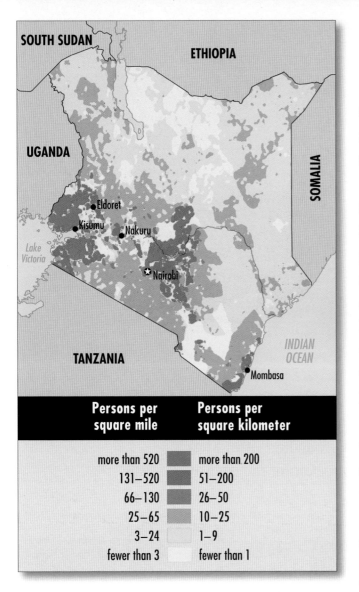

Persons per square mile	Persons per square kilometer
more than 520	more than 200
131–520	51–200
66–130	26–50
25–65	10–25
3–24	1–9
fewer than 3	fewer than 1

Major cities (2009 est.)

Nairobi	3,375,000
Mombasa	1,200,000
Kisumu	409,928
Nakuru	307,990
Eldoret	289,380

and along the coast. The dry desert regions of the north and east are sparsely settled.

Kenya has one of the world's fastest rates of population growth. Since independence in 1963, the population has grown from eight million to forty-five million. The country's high birth rate means Kenya's population is young—about 40 percent are fourteen years old or younger. Only about 3 percent of Kenyans are age sixty-five or older.

Kenya has a lower life expectancy than much of the world. The average life span for a Kenyan man is sixty-two years. For a woman, it is sixty-five years. Many Kenyans do not have access to clean drinking water, so disease spreads easily. Kenya also has one of the world's highest rates of the disease AIDS.

Ethnic Groups

Most Kenyans identify with one of the country's many ethnic groups. The population of these ethnic groups varies greatly. The largest, the Kikuyu, account for nearly one-quarter of the country's population of just over forty-five million. The

Like other world capitals, Nairobi has important government buildings and modern transportation and communications systems. But within the city is a poor neighborhood called Kibera. It was originally a suburb of Nairobi, founded by Sudanese soldiers who fought for the British in World War I. Now it is sometimes called a city within a city. Hundreds of thousands of people currently live in Kibera, an area of just under 1 square mile (2.6 sq km)—about the size of New York City's Central Park. Many Kenyans come to Nairobi from rural areas looking for work. When they can't find jobs, they end up in Kibera. Until recently, there was no freshwater in the neighborhood, and disease is common. In 2009, the Kenyan government began moving people out of Kibera and into new apartments in Nairobi. Some residents resisted, including descendants of the original Sudanese founders, who claim to own much of the land in Kibera. The fate of the neighborhood is uncertain.

smallest ethnic group, the El Molo, has fewer than one thousand members.

The Kikuyu traditionally lived in the region around Mount Kenya. Many Kikuyu people lost their land to white settlers during the colonial era, so the community spread to other parts of the country. Today, some Kikuyu still farm in their traditional region.

The next largest group is the Luhya, who are centered near Lake Victoria and Mount Elgon. They were traditionally farmers, and today many grow tea and corn. Also living near Lake

Diverse People **91**

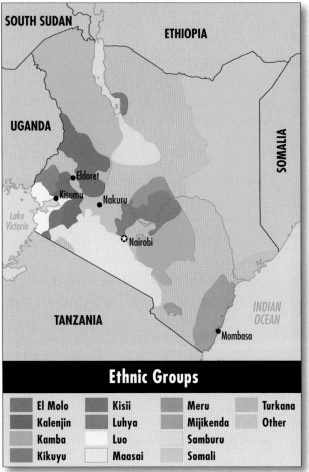

Ethnic Groups

El Molo	Kisii	Meru	Turkana
Kalenjin	Luhya	Mijikenda	Other
Kamba	Luo	Samburu	
Kikuyu	Maasai	Somali	

Kenya's Ethnic Groups

Kikuyu	22%
Luhya	14%
Luo	13%
Kalenjin	12%
Kamba	11%
Kisii	6%
Meru	6%
Other Africans	15%
Non-African (Asian, European, and Arab)	1%

Victoria are the Luo. Along with growing crops, the Luo fish the lake's waters.

Like the Kikuyu and the Luo, the Kalenjin have played a major role in Kenya's politics since independence. The Kalenjin group includes a number of smaller groups that speak a similar language and came together to work for their shared political interests. Most Kalenjin live on the western side of the Rift Valley.

One of Kenya's smaller but best-known groups is the Maasai. Their homeland is in the grasslands of southern Kenya, where they herd cattle, goats, and sheep. Their lands once extended farther north, until the British arrived and took some of it away.

Closely related to the Maasai are the Samburu, who live on the plains north of Mount Kenya. Both Maasai and Samburu move to a few different regions during the year to follow the rains and find grazing land for their herds. These herding communities have developed an intimate knowledge of the environment, so they know how to find grass and water for their herds in a very dry place. Because they have to move every few months, they build homes with local materials and they often just take the foundation of their house with them when they leave.

From Beyond Kenya's Borders

When Kenya gained independence, about fifty-six thousand people of European descent lived there. Most had ties to Great Britain or South Africa, another former British colony. After 1963, most of the whites gradually left the country.

A Samburu man performs a traditional jumping dance.

Becoming an Adult

Rites of passage are important in many of Kenya's communities. Among the Maasai, older men take young teenage boys into their care for several weeks to teach them the responsibilities of being an adult. Then, there is a big ceremony where the boys graduate to adulthood. Each group of boys is given a name. This name acts like a bond of friendship among the boys and they maintain these close ties as they grow older.

Diverse People **93**

Workers deliver bags of food to a Somali refugee camp in northeastern Kenya.

British colonial rule had brought another large group of foreign people to Kenya. Great Britain once also ruled India, and it sent workers from India to build Kenya's railroad. Other Indians came to work as merchants.

In recent years, problems in Somalia and Sudan have led tens of thousands of people to leave those countries and settle in Kenya. Some of them live in refugee camps in northern Kenya. Others have settled in Nairobi. Kenyans with Somali ethnic roots dominate a neighborhood in Nairobi called Eastleigh.

Education

Children in Kenya begin attending school at age six. The school year starts in January and runs through November. School usually begins between 7:00 and 8:00 a.m., and typically ends between 3:30 and 5:00 p.m. Children are required to go to school through eighth grade. At the end of eighth grade, students take an exam to obtain a Kenyan Certificate of Primary Education. This exam covers Swahili, English, mathematics and agriculture, science, and social studies. The results of this exam determine which secondary school, or high school, students will go to. High school lasts four years. Many students who do well in high school continue on to university.

Kenya has about fifty universities. The University of Nairobi is the oldest and largest, serving about sixty thousand students.

In the first three years of school in Kenya, classes are taught in Swahili. In later years, English is the primary language used in schools.

CHAPTER 8

A Spiritual Path

IN CHURCHES, MOSQUES, TEMPLES, AND OUTDOORS, Kenyans take part in a variety of religious ceremonies. Some Kenyans hold beliefs that have their roots in older African traditions. But today, the vast majority of Kenyans belong to Christian churches, with a minority following Islam. Some Kenyans combine Christianity or Islam with traditional African beliefs.

Opposite: **A Catholic woman prays during a mass in central Kenya. Catholic missionaries first came to Kenya in the late 1800s.**

Traditional Religions

Given Kenya's cultural diversity, their traditional practices take many forms. Like other religions, traditional Kenyan religions are concerned with issues such as how the world was created and how humans are supposed to live. The religions explain the relationship between people and the world around them, and between people and the spiritual world.

Maasai men exchange greetings over a sacrificed cow.

Many of Kenya's traditional religions are monotheistic. This means the people believe in just one god. Different peoples have different names for this god who created the

The First People

When Christians tell the story of the origin of humanity, they talk about Adam and Eve in the Garden of Eden. Similarly, many African communities have stories about the first people on earth. According to traditional Kikuyu belief, the god Ngai created the first man, Gikuyu (another name for the Kikuyu). Ngai told Gikuyu the land would belong to him and his children. Gikuyu soon went to a forest of fig trees and found a beautiful woman named Mumbi. Gikuyu and Mumbi had nine daughters. The daughters needed husbands. Following Ngai's instructions, the daughters found sticks and brought them to their father, who used them to build a fire. Out of the fire walked nine men who became the daughters' husbands.

Today, Kikuyu people believe they can all trace their heritage back to one of these original ancestors. Some still name their daughters for Mumbi and her nine daughters, whose names all begin with W. This gives the people in the Kikuyu community a feeling of being part of one big extended family. Nobel Peace Prize–winner Wangari Maathai was named for one of the daughters.

The Kayas of Coastal Kenya

Along the coast of Kenya are the remains of about thirty Mijikenda forest villages called kayas. The Mijikenda started building these villages during the 1500s. By the 1940s, however, the people left the villages for new homes in larger towns and cities. Today, the Mijikenda consider the kayas sacred sites because their ancestors are buried there. They think of the kayas as the homes of their dead relatives. In 2008, the United Nations Educational, Scientific and Cultural Organization (UNESCO) named the kayas a World Heritage Site, a place of outstanding cultural or natural significance, which means the kayas will be preserved. The Mijikenda people still maintain the sites and perform rituals there (left).

universe or has control over the natural world. The Maasai and related communities call their god Engai or Ngai. One way the Maasai and other animal herders honor their god is by killing a goat or sheep—a valuable piece of property.

In many traditional religions, Mount Kenya is a sacred place. The god in the traditional religions of the Kikuyu, who also call their god Ngai, is said to live on the mountain peak.

The Kikuyu, like other Kenyans, honor the spirits of dead relatives. They don't worship them as gods, but they do believe deceased ancestors can influence the lives of the living. This is similar to how saints are viewed in the Catholic Church. To honor grandparents, newborns are sometimes named for them. This practice goes on even in cities, where traditional religions are seldom practiced.

Practicing Muslims pray five times a day.

Religions of Kenya (2009)	
Protestant	47.4%
Roman Catholic	23.3%
Other Christian faiths	11.8%
Muslim	11.1%
Traditional religions	1.6%
Other	1.7%
None	2.4%
Unspecified	0.7%

Islam Then and Now

Islam arrived in what is now Kenya more than one thousand years ago, with traders who sailed to the Kenyan coast. Kenyans also went to the Arabian Peninsula and began to embrace the messages that Islam taught. Islam remained the major religion along the coast through the rule of the Omani sultans. The faith spread farther inland when the British began building settlements along the railway. Today, Muslims are found throughout the country, though most still live along the coast and in Somali communities.

Most Muslim men in Kenya today wear white caps called *kofia* to indicate their faith. Many women wear a head covering called a *hijab*. Muslim children often attend special schools to learn Arabic, at the end of the regular school day. Islam's holy book, the Qur'an, is written in Arabic.

A Major Mosque

Jamia Mosque is the largest mosque in Nairobi. Standing in the city's central business area, it is notable for its three silver domes and tall twin minarets, which are towers attached to mosques. The call to prayer, announcing that it is time for Muslims to pray, is broadcast from the minarets. Plans for building Jamia Mosque began in 1902, and construction took more than thirty years. A new wing was added in 1998.

Christians Arrive

Christians came to Kenya much later than the Muslims. The first Protestant missionaries arrived from Germany in the nineteenth century. They were soon followed by missionaries from Great Britain. The missionaries converted some people and then encouraged them to go across the country to seek more converts. The missionaries also built some schools and hospitals.

Not all Kenyans were converted by Christian missionaries in their own country. The Luo often traveled into the area that became Uganda. Christian missionaries reached there before they came to the Luo homelands in Kenya. The Luo learned Christianity from their neighbors and then passed along their knowledge when they returned home. When the missionaries finally reached the Luo corner of Kenya, they asked the Luo to help them spread Christian teachings.

Most Africans adopted Christianity through the teachings of other Africans. For instance, one young man might go to a mission school. After he graduated, he would return home and start his own church. Knowing the local language, African missionaries were well equipped to spread Christianity among the larger population. This gave Africans a lot of power in shaping how Christianity was adopted locally. It also led to the creation of many local churches that mixed traditional African beliefs with mainstream Christian faiths.

The number of different Protestant faiths in Kenya grew during the twentieth century. Today, Protestants in Kenya include Anglicans, Methodists, Lutherans, Baptists, and Presbyterians. Other Christians are Quakers or members of Pentecostal churches. Pentecostals believe that God, through the Holy Spirit, can send people messages or help cure the sick.

The single largest faith in Kenya is Roman Catholicism. The pope, the leader of the Roman Catholic Church, sent missionaries to Zanzibar in 1860, and others soon reached the East African mainland.

In recent years, tens of thousands of Kenyans have joined a church called the Ecumenical Catholic Church of Christ. Unlike the Roman Catholic Church, its leaders believe that Catholic priests should be allowed to marry. The first African

A Kenyan Martyr

Around 1870, the German missionary Johannes Rebmann taught a young Kenyan named David Koi (?–1883) about Christianity. Koi became a missionary himself. He worked among people who had escaped slavery and lived near Takaungu, on the coast. In 1879, he started a community for fugitives from slavery at Fuladoyo, northwest of Mombasa. Koi converted to Christianity the people who arrived at his community. Over the next several years, hundreds of people fled to Fuladoyo, seeking safety from their masters. Koi's missionary work angered nearby Muslim leaders. They killed him in 1883, making Koi the first Kenyan Christian martyr—a person who is murdered for his or her religious beliefs.

leader of the church was a Kenyan, Godfrey Shiundu Wasike.

The Orthodox Church, which was once united with the Roman Catholic Church, also has a presence in Kenya. Greek immigrants started the first Orthodox church in Kenya at the beginning of the twentieth century. The Coptic Orthodox Church, an Orthodox Christian church with its roots in Egypt, also has followers in Kenya. The Copts opened their first church in Nairobi in 1976 and today have almost thirty churches.

Asian Faiths

The Indians who came to Kenya with the British brought their religions with them. Some Indians were Muslims, but a larger number were Hindus, the most common faith in India. The Hindu Council of Kenya supports the interests of all Hindus and has offices in Nairobi and several other cities. Other religions with roots in India that are found in Kenya are Sikhism and Jainism.

Hindus fill the streets of Nairobi during a festival. Most Hindu Kenyans are of Asian descent.

CHAPTER 9

Arts and Sports

FOR CENTURIES, LOCAL CRAFTSPEOPLE IN KENYA have made everyday items of great beauty. Sometimes their work has had religious importance. Carved wooden masks, for example, represented ancestors. Adding hair and jewelry to the masks was a sign of respect. Other masks represented spirits. Kenyan artists still make masks for their own use and to sell to tourists.

Opposite: **A Maasai man displays a carved wooden mask.**

Crafts

The Kamba, some say, are the most skilled carvers in Kenya. Along with making bowls and wooden jewelry, some Kamba carve animals. The Kamba believe their god shapes the form of all living things. By taking a raw piece of wood and giving it a distinct shape, the carvers are honoring their god's work. The carvers of Lamu are known for their chests, which come in many sizes. They also make carved doors that are common along the coast.

Maasai women make elaborate beaded jewelry. Each color is symbolic. For example, red represents bravery and strength.

Jewelry making is another time-honored craft in Kenya. Kenyans make jewelry out of metal, wood, and beads. Jewelers often use brass and copper, but some even use the metal from old aluminum pots. The Maasai are known for their colorful beaded jewelry. The color and arrangement of the beads can indicate a person's position in society or relationship to a particular group. Beadwork is traditionally done by women. Some Kenyans also make baskets from fibers such as sisal.

Modern Art

Kenya's earliest artists and craftspeople were largely self-taught or learned from family members. Today, many Kenyans go to school to learn about painting. The art they create often blends traditional subjects with influences from other parts of the world.

One of Kenya's best-known artists is Kivuthi Mbuno. Using ink and sometimes crayons, he creates scenes of animals in the wild or people carrying out their daily activities. Meek Gichugu was just twenty-two when he caught the attention of the art world in 1991. His paintings are almost like being inside a dream, as nothing in his paintings looks quite like it does in real life.

Traditional Music and Dance

For many Kenyans, dancing is more than something to do for fun. Dance defines their culture. The Maasai and other com-

Preserving the Old Ways

As president, Jomo Kenyatta urged Kenyans to keep their traditional forms of music and dance. Kenyatta said, "Dance is the mirror of our life and beyond. It reflects...our dialogue with the past and our present feelings and thoughts." In 1971, the government created a special performance space called the Bomas of Kenya in Nairobi. There, members of different ethnic groups play traditional music for visitors or perform for Kenyan schoolchildren to teach them about the country's cultural diversity. A group called the Harambee Dancers performs dances from across the country.

munities are known for the *adumu*, or jumping dance. Young men sing while a few of them jump as high as they can in a circle. Other dances mark such events as a wedding or the killing of a lion. Dancing and singing are also common in church services and as a way to welcome a guest into a community.

Traditional instruments played across Kenya include wooden drums, horns made from animal horns or large gourds, and string instruments with one to eight strings. Singing with or without instruments is important to many Kenyans. They sing special songs at weddings or while doing work. Some herders near Lake Turkana make up songs for their favorite oxen. Children sometimes sing songs about the wildlife around them.

A Kisii man plays a traditional eight-string lyre called an obokano. Plucking the strings produces a buzzing sound.

Making Modern Music

Musicians in Kenya have been influenced by music from many sources. At times, they have blended Kenyan music with styles from other parts of Africa, Europe, and North and South America. Some styles of popular music are connected to a particular region, and fans often follow the careers of musicians from the same ethnic group as their own.

One musical style popular across Kenya is *benga*. It was started by Luo musicians who took music once played on traditional string instruments and adapted it for electric guitar. A lead guitarist plays along with a singer, all to a fast beat. Another type of music with wide appeal is *taarab*. The songs are sung in Swahili, so most people can understand them, and the lyrics are about the experiences of daily life: death, love, and happy occasions.

Benga music mixes traditional rhythms and rumba beats. The use of acoustic instruments in this music eventually gave way to electric instruments.

Young people in Kenya listen to artists from around the world, especially African American hip-hop and rhythm and blues performers. Today, native Kenyans are becoming stars playing those same musical styles. Women singers have become popular, such as the hip-hop star Nazizi.

Kenyan hip-hop artists often use the language of the youth population in their songs. Young people in Nairobi commonly speak a hybrid of English, Swahili, and local languages. The mixture of these languages is called Sheng (Swahili-English). Sheng has now become a popular language for young people in other cities and is used by many popular musicians.

Jua Cali is one of Kenya's most popular hip-hop stars. He performs in both Swahili and Sheng.

Creativity with Words

Before Europeans came to Kenya, people told stories, rather than writing them down. Books about Kenya became common during the colonial era, but most were written by Europeans or Americans and presented a foreign viewpoint that sometimes looked down on Africans. Still, these books gave many people outside Africa a picture of the scenery and people of Kenya.

Kenyans who learned English sometimes wrote in that language. One such person was Jomo Kenyatta. In 1938, he published *Facing Mount Kenya*, a book about how the Kikuyu lived before the British arrived. After Kenya gained independence, more writers emerged. One of the best was Ngugi wa Thiong'o, who wrote several novels describing the struggle of average Kenyans before and after independence. A later

Ngugi wa Thiong'o published his first novel in 1964. In the late 1970s, Kenyan officials imprisoned him for the political nature of his work. After his release, he moved to the United States.

From Medicine to Writing

After finishing at the top of her high school class, Margaret Ogola (1958–2011) went to college in Nairobi to study medicine. By 1990 she had earned two degrees and seemed set on a career as a children's doctor. But along the way Ogola also found time to write a novel about Kenyan women, *The River and the Source*. The book won a national prize for literature, as did her 2007 book *Place of Destiny*. The fame from her writing did not keep Ogola from her medical work, as she led several organizations, including one to fight the spread of HIV and AIDS in children. Ogola wrote both *Place of Destiny* and her last book, *Mandate of the People*, while fighting her own health battle against cancer. She submitted her last manuscript to her publisher just before she died.

Lupita Nyong'o

writer who tackled some of the same issues is David Mulwa. His best-known book is *Master and Servant*.

Film and Television

In 2014, the Kenyan actor Lupita Nyong'o won an Academy Award, the highest honor in the U.S. film industry, for her performance in the film *12 Years a Slave*. She was the first Kenyan to win an Academy Award. Although Nyong'o has done some film work in Kenya, most of her work has been in the United States. Her success, though, brought new attention to filmmaking in Kenya.

Some foreign films have been shot in Kenya, such as the popular film *Out of Africa*. But few movies have been made by Kenyans themselves. The government is now trying to change that. The Kenya Film Commission is working to build a school to train local filmmakers. Finding an audience, though, can be hard. People in rural areas don't have access to theaters, and going to the movies is a luxury many people in cities cannot afford.

Kenya also has a television industry, and some Kenyan companies create original shows for it. Other shows come from Europe, the United States, or South Africa. Kenyan television is similar to what viewers see in North America, with news, talks shows, and entertainment. One popular TV figure is Julie Gichuru. Trained as a lawyer, she is the host of a successful TV news show.

Julie Gichuru (left) is one of the most popular TV journalists in Kenya.

Soccer is wildly popular in Kenya. These children do not have a soccer ball, so they are playing with a ball made out of plastic bags tied with string.

Sports

As in many countries, some of the most popular TV broadcasts in Kenya involve sports. Kenyans love to watch soccer, known there as football, and kids love to play it. Some Kenyan soccer players have joined top European teams. Two other popular sports, cricket and rugby, also arrived in Kenya from Great Britain. Kenyans enjoy watching boxing, and basketball is growing in popularity.

Kenya is one of eight African nations that host an auto race that is part of the African Rally Championship. Kenya's Safari Rally was first held in 1953. Drivers race specially made cars over the rough, rural roads, sometimes hitting bumps that send them airborne. One local driver who excelled in the rally was Joginder Singh. He won three times between 1965 and 1976.

In the world of international sports, Kenya is known for producing some of the world's best long-distance runners. In particular, Kalenjins from western Kenya dominate marathon races. The first Kenyan runner to win a gold medal in the Summer Olympics was Kip Keino in 1968. At the 2012 games, twelve Kenyan men and women won medals in a variety of running events.

The World's Fastest

As a teenager, Dennis Kimetto (1984–) went to the community center in his local village to watch Kenyan runners such as Paul Tergat compete. Kimetto's family farmed, and they did not have a television at home. Kimetto was inspired by Kenya's many extraordinary runners. He

hoped to one day compete at their level, but he needed to help his family, so he, too, worked as a farmer.

Kimetto did not begin training seriously until 2008. One day, he encountered Geoffrey Mutai, one of the world's top marathoners, who was training near his home. At 26.2 miles (42.2 km), the marathon is the longest commonly run road race in the world. Mutai was impressed by Kimetto's skill and invited him to join his training camp. Kimetto's career quickly took off. By 2011, he was winning races. The following year, he came in second at the Berlin Marathon in Germany, trailing his running partner, Mutai.

Then, in 2014, Kimetto moved ahead of his mentor. In Berlin, Kimetto broke the world record in the marathon, completing the race in 2 hours, 2 minutes, 57 seconds. That was twenty-six seconds faster than the previous world record. Never before had anyone run a marathon in under 2 hours, 3 minutes. With this feat, Kimetto added his name to the list of great Kenyan long-distance runners.

CHAPTER 10

Daily Life

THE TYPICAL DAY OF KENYANS VARIES GREATLY ACROSS the country. The life of Maasai herders tending cattle in the grasslands is nothing like the fast-paced routines people follow in the business district of Nairobi. Finding enough healthy food to eat every day can be a challenge for Kenyans in the desert north. And daily practices can be deeply shaped by religion, as with the Muslims who live along the coast.

Opposite: **A man drives a herd of cattle in southern Kenya. There are about fourteen million head of cattle in Kenya.**

Village Life

Members of Kenya's many different rural communities share many day-to-day practices. Wives take care of the household, raise the children, and grow crops. Men often work outside the village, if jobs are available, and take care of livestock, hunt or fish, and run the local village government. Women have direct control over the money they earn from selling crops or other goods. Likewise, men have control over the money they make from their work.

A mother in Malindi with her children. On average, Kenyan women have three or four children.

Families include more people than just parents and their children. Sometimes, the father's parents live with the family as well, and many people live close to other relatives.

After giving birth, mothers traditionally carry their children strapped to their backs as they go about their day. This

Seeking a Wife

In some rural areas of Kenya, a woman's family plays a role in her marriage proposal. For example, in the Kikuyu culture, a man goes to the village of his girl-friend and announces he wants to marry her. Then someone representing the man's family brings gifts to the woman's family. If the woman is interested in the man, she says so, and then the two families arrange for the bridewealth. This is money, livestock, or goods that the man's family gives to the woman's family. At the wedding, friends and family come together to celebrate. As part of the ceremony, the groom feeds his bride a piece of meat from an animal killed for the occasion. When the day is done, the bride moves in with her new husband's family.

Let's Play

A popular game for Kenyans of all ages is *mbao*. Different forms of the game are played across Africa and beyond, and the names and rules vary. In the United States, it is often known as mancala. In mbao, two players sit across from each other with a wooden board between them. The board has two rows of holes. The holes can also be dug into the dirt or carved into rocks. The players start with an equal number of seeds and place them in the row of holes closet to them. On each turn, the players take all the seeds in one hole and place them in other holes, one at a time and in clockwise order. If the last seed lands in an opponent's hole, the first player captures all the seeds in it. The two players take turns moving the seeds until one player does not have any seeds left in the holes on his or her side. The player who has captured the most seeds at that point wins.

practice continues until the children are old enough to walk. Once the children can walk, they usually stay with their mothers as the women work. Young children sometimes get to play on their own. Just as in North America, children enjoy playing hide-and-seek or pretending to be adults.

As girls get older, they help their mothers take care of the younger siblings. In some areas, women have to spend several hours every day walking to a well to retrieve clean water. The older girls help with this and other tasks, such as collecting firewood. They also learn how to make clothing and jewelry. As boys grow older, they spend more time with their fathers. Among the Maasai, the boys copy what the older men do, using a stick to pretend to herd cattle.

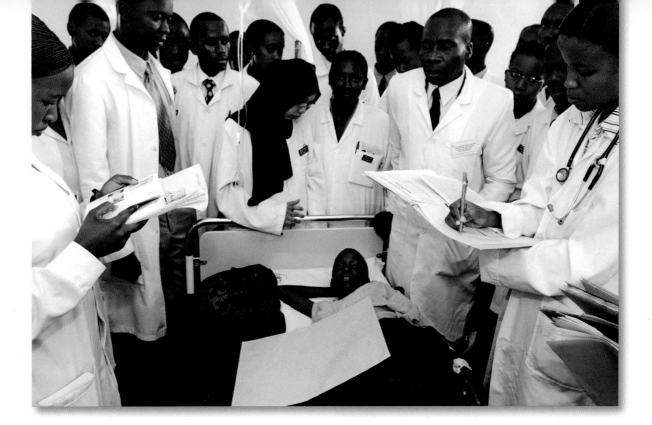

Women now make up about 44 percent of university students in Kenya. As they gain access to education, an increasing number of Kenyan women are entering fields such as medicine.

City Life

Compared to village life, a typical day is much different for urban Kenyans. Often both parents have jobs outside the home, so children do not spend as much time with their parents as village children do. Women are more likely to be educated and have fewer children than rural women have. At times, though, families struggle to pay for the uniforms and fees required to send children to school. Students who do well in their elementary schooling can win scholarships to attend high school.

City dwellers live in a variety of homes. The richest people live in large homes behind gates in the suburbs of Nairobi. The poorest live in small shacks made of mud and concrete in neighborhoods like Kibera. These families cram into a single, small space, with some people sleeping on the floor.

Houses in Kenya

In the wealthy areas of Kenyan cities, the houses are similar to large ones in North America. But in the rural areas there are much simpler buildings. The materials available in a region influence how houses are built. Some homes are made out of mud or concrete, while others are made from wood or grass. The floors of the buildings might be dirt, though some are concrete. In the past, roofs were usually made of plant material, but many are now made of tin. And in some places, people are building homes out of cement rather than the traditional materials.

Most houses are made up of a series of small, separate buildings around an open area. Each building is used for its own purpose, such as cooking or sleeping. Since most rural Kenyans cook over an open fire, they need a separate house to cook in so that the smoke does not go throughout the home's living areas. Parents and their children usually sleep in a building separate from where the grandparents sleep.

The streets of the cities are lined with merchants selling such things as firewood for cooking, fruits and vegetables, and DVDs of movies. Along with cars, minivans and buses called *matatus* rumble through the city streets. In some coastal communities, people take *tuk tuks* to go from place to place. These three-wheeled motorcycles can carry three passengers.

Dress for the Occasion

People who work in Kenya's cities or government offices tend to dress as North Americans do. Men wear jackets and ties, and women wear suits or blouses and pants or skirts.

On the Road

As in other countries that were colonies of Great Britain in the twentieth century, Kenyans drive on the left side of the road. In the United States, Canada, and the majority of other countries, cars are driven on the right. Kenyan drivers can seem a little daring—or reckless—to visitors, as they pass each other at fast speeds. Outside of main cities, roads are not in good condition, and many are not paved. Driving at night can be hard, too, as many roads do not have signs and many cars are missing headlights.

In rural areas, people tend to wear cloth wraps that cover most of their body. Urban residents might wear something similar when they're at home. Young people often wear jeans and T-shirts.

Many people in Kenyan cities dress similarly to people in North America.

Certain cultures are associated with certain types of clothing. The Maasai are known for their bright red *shukas*, blankets of cotton cloth that tie around the waist and sometimes cover one shoulder. In the warmer areas of the country, some men wear *kanzus*. This long, white cotton shirt covers most of the body and is associated with the Swahili culture.

Meals and Celebrations

In rural areas, people eat whatever crops they grow. They might also buy some fruits and vegetables at a local market. People who live near Lake Victoria or close to the Indian Ocean eat plenty of fish. People in the coastal regions often

Clothing with a Message

All over the world, people wear T-shirts with slogans and messages on them. Some Kenyan women put messages on a different article of clothing, a wrap called a *kanga*. The kanga was first created in Zanzibar when seamstresses sewed together handkerchiefs of different patterns and colors. Women wore them wrapped around their body, sometimes adding a second kanga to cover their head. Kangas spread to the Swahili of Kenya and can now be seen across the country. Putting proverbs on kangas is a recent practice. A kanga with a message is called a *leso*. People who give kangas as gifts choose a message appropriate for the occasion or recipient. The message might remind a pregnant woman how hard it is to raise a child, or it might remind the recipient of the power of love.

prepare foods that reflect Asian and Middle Eastern cultural influences. Chapati, an Indian flatbread, is common there, as is curry. Many of the foods influenced by Indian cooking are available across the country.

In the highlands people often eat *irio*, which is a mixture of corn, potatoes, and sometimes peas. Another food based on corn or other local grains such as millet is *ugali*. The grain is mixed with water and cooked until it turns into a thick dough. Diners break off pieces of the ugali and use it to scoop up vegetables. If they can afford it, Kenyans enjoy roasted meat, called *nyama choma*. People who herd livestock occasionally kill some of their animals for meat, but most of their diet comes from dairy products made from their animals' milk.

A market in Mombasa. Kenyans eat a wide variety of vegetables, including tomatoes, peppers, and sweet potatoes.

Making Ugali

Ugali is a cornmeal dish Kenyans eat with many meals. It has only two ingredients, but getting the texture just right takes practice. Have an adult help you with this recipe.

Ingredients

4 cups water   2 cups white cornmeal

Directions

Put the water in a large pot over high heat, and bring the water to a boil. Turn down the heat to medium and slowly add the cornmeal, stirring it with a whisk to remove lumps. Keep stirring while the cornmeal cooks, adding more cornmeal to make it thicker. This can take up to 20 minutes. The cornmeal is done when it pulls away from the sides of the pot.

Let the ugali cool a few minutes. Then put a plate on top of the pot and turn the pot upside down so the ugali drops out. It should be thick enough to cut with a knife. Serve with any meat, vegetables, or sauce you choose.

Kenya's National Holidays

New Year's Day	January 1
Good Friday	March or April
Easter Monday	March or April
Labor Day	May 1
Madaraka Day (anniversary of self-rule)	June 1
Mashujaa Day (Heroes' Day)	October 20
Independence Day	December 12
Christmas	December 25
Boxing Day	December 26
Idd ul Fitr (end of Ramadan)	Date varies

In cities and towns, people can buy food at outdoor markets or at stores. They can also buy some foods from street vendors. Kenyans enjoy a stew made with beans, corn, and sometimes meat. Vendors cook it in large pots called *sufurias*. Other street sellers offer roasted corn and fried yams. In the largest cities, people who can afford it can dine at restaurants offering food from many different countries.

When washing down their food, Kenyans often reach for locally grown tea. Tea is sometimes brewed with milk and sugar already in the water. Although Kenya produces a great deal of coffee, most of it is exported. It is not popular in Kenya. Along the Indian Ocean, Kenyans enjoy drinking coconut milk.

Just as people around the world do, Kenyans celebrate special occasions with large feasts. They typically roast an entire animal, such as an ox or goat. Elders or guests are given the best cuts of meat. Even the blood of the animals is used as food. For the Maasai, one of their special dishes is cow's blood cooked with milk.

Kenyans find pleasure in their art, culture, families, and celebrations, as they work to brighten the future of their country.

Honoring the Dead

Though a funeral is a sad occasion, for Kenyans it is also a time for the living to come together for a feast and celebration of the deceased person's life. Traditionally, when someone dies, family members take the body back to their community's region, so the dead person can be buried near ancestors. A parade of cars and trucks brings relatives to the burial plot, which is often on the person's family farm. The people tie red ribbons to the vehicles to indicate they are part of a funeral procession. After the burial, the people gather to listen to music, talk, and eat. The Luo are known for very large funeral events. Guests might stay for several weeks, as the family of the person provides them meals. That tradition, though, is changing. Many Kenyans are finding it hard to pay for the kind of funerals most guests expect.

Timeline

KENYAN HISTORY		WORLD HISTORY	
Hominids begin making tools near Lake Turkana.	ca. 2 million years ago		
Cushitic-speaking people reach what is now Kenya.	ca. 2000 BCE	ca. 2500 BCE	The Egyptians build the pyramids and the Sphinx in Giza.
		ca. 563 BCE	The Buddha is born in India.
Foreign traders reach the Kenyan coast.	100–400 CE	313 CE	The Roman emperor Constantine legalizes Christianity.
		610	The Prophet Muhammad begins preaching a new religion called Islam.
Mombasa is founded.	ca. 900		
The Swahili language and culture arise.	ca. 1000	1054	The Eastern (Orthodox) and Western (Roman Catholic) Churches break apart.
		1095	The Crusades begin.
		1215	King John seals the Magna Carta.
		1300s	The Renaissance begins in Italy.
		1347	The plague sweeps through Europe.
		1453	Ottoman Turks capture Constantinople, conquering the Byzantine Empire.
		1492	Columbus arrives in North America.
Portuguese explorer Vasco da Gama reaches Kenya.	1498	1500s	Reformers break away from the Catholic Church, and Protestantism is born.
The Portuguese sack Mombasa.	1505		
The Portuguese begin building Fort Jesus in Mombasa.	1592		
Muhammad Yusif bin Hassan leads a revolt against the Portuguese.	1631		
Omani and Kenyan forces defeat the Portuguese in Mombasa.	1698		
The Portuguese leave Kenya.	1729		
		1776	The U.S. Declaration of Independence is signed.
		1789	The French Revolution begins.

KENYAN HISTORY

Omani sultan Seyyid Said unites Swahili lands under his rule.	**Early 1800s**
German Johann Krapf becomes the first European missionary to go to Kenya.	**ca. 1844**
European countries begin dividing up Africa; Great Britain receives lands that include Kenya.	**1884–1885**
The British begin building a railway across Kenya.	**1895**
Slavery is abolished in Kenya.	**1907**
Kenyans supporting independence form the Kenya African Union.	**1944**
The Mau Mau rebellion begins.	**1952**
Kenya wins independence.	**1963**
Kenya becomes a republic; Jomo Kenyatta is elected president.	**1964**
Jomo Kenyatta dies; Daniel arap Moi becomes president.	**1978**
Multiparty elections are allowed for the first time in decades.	**1992**
Terrorists bomb the U.S. embassy in Nairobi.	**1998**
Mwai Kibaki is elected president.	**2002**
Wangari Maathai wins the Nobel Peace Prize.	**2004**
Violence erupts after a disputed presidential election.	**2007**
Kenyans approve a new constitution.	**2010**
Oil is discovered in northern Kenya.	**2012**
Uhuru Kenyatta is elected president.	**2013**

WORLD HISTORY

1865	The American Civil War ends.
1879	The first practical lightbulb is invented.
1914	World War I begins.
1917	The Bolshevik Revolution brings communism to Russia.
1929	A worldwide economic depression begins.
1939	World War II begins.
1945	World War II ends.
1969	Humans land on the Moon.
1975	The Vietnam War ends.
1989	The Berlin Wall is torn down as communism crumbles in Eastern Europe.
1991	The Soviet Union breaks into separate states.
2001	Terrorists attack the World Trade Center in New York City and the Pentagon near Washington, D.C.
2004	A tsunami in the Indian Ocean destroys coastlines in Africa, India, and Southeast Asia.
2008	The United States elects its first African American president.

Fast Facts

Official name: Republic of Kenya

Capital: Nairobi

Official languages: Swahili, English

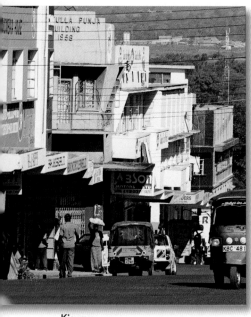

Kisumu

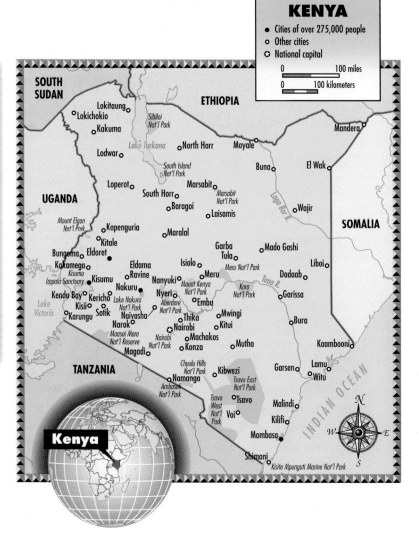

KENYA

- Cities of over 275,000 people
- Other cities
- National capital

0   100 miles
0   100 kilometers

SOUTH SUDAN

Lokitaung
Lokichokio
Kakuma
Lodwar

ETHIOPIA

Sibiloi Nat'l Park
Lake Turkana
North Horr
Moyale
Mandera

South Island Nat'l Park
Buna
El Wak

UGANDA

Loperot
South Horr
Baragoi
Marsabit
Marsabit Nat'l Park
Laisamis
Wajir

SOMALIA

Laga Bor R.

Mount Elgon Nat'l Prk
Kapenguria
Kitale
Maralal
Garba Tula
Mado Gashi
Liboi

Bungoma
Kakamega
Eldoret
Eldama Ravine
Isiolo
Meru
Meru Nat'l Park
Dadaab

Kisumu
Impala Sanctuary
Kisumu
Nakuru
Nanyuki
Mount Kenya Nat'l Park
Kora Nat'l Park
Tana R.
Garissa

Kendu Bay
Kisii
Kericho
Lake Nakuru Nat'l Park
Nyeri
Aberdare Nat'l Park
Embu
Mwingi
Bura

Lake Victoria
Karungu
Sotik
Naivasha
Thika
Kitui

Narok
Nairobi
Machakos
Kaambooni

Maasai Mara Nat'l Reserve
Nairobi Nat'l Park
Konza
Mutha

Magadi

TANZANIA

Chyulu Hills Nat'l Park
Kibwezi
Garsen
Lamu
Witu

Namanga
Amboseli Nat'l Park
Tsavo East Nat'l Park

Tsavo West Nat'l Park
Tsavo
Voi
Malindi
Kilifi

INDIAN OCEAN

Mombasa

Shimoni
Kisite Mpunguti Marine Nat'l Park

Kenya

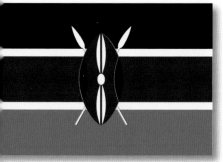

National flag

Gura Falls

Official religion:	None
Founding date:	June 1, 1963, obtained internal self-rule; full independence from Great Britain granted on December 12, 1963
National anthem:	"Ee Mungu Nguvu Yetu" ("O God of All Creation")
Type of government:	Republic
Head of state:	President
Head of government:	President
Area of country:	224,960 square miles (582,644 sq km)
Latitude and longitude of geographic center:	1°00' N, 38°00' E
Bordering countries:	Somalia to the east, Ethiopia and South Sudan to the north, Uganda to the west, and Tanzania to the south
Highest elevation:	Mount Kenya, 17,058 feet (5,199 m) above sea level
Lowest elevation:	Sea level along the Indian Ocean
Average high temperature:	In Nairobi, 80°F (27°C) in March, 73°F (23°C) in August; in Mombasa, 91°F (33°C) in March, 83°F (28°C) in August
Average low temperature:	In Nairobi, 54°F (12°C) in March, 48°F (9°C) in August; in Mombasa, 76°F (24°C) in March, 69°F (21°C) in August
Average annual precipitation:	In Nairobi, 42 inches (107 cm)

Mount Kenya

National population (2014 est.):	45,010,056	
Population of major cities (2009 est.):	Nairobi	3,375,000
	Mombasa	1,200,000
	Kisumu	409,928
	Nakuru	307,990
	Eldoret	289,380

Landmarks:
- ▶ *Fort Jesus*, Mombasa
- ▶ *Maasai Mara National Reserve*, near Tanzanian border
- ▶ *Mount Kenya*, Nyeri
- ▶ *Nairobi National Museum*, Nairobi
- ▶ *Nairobi National Park*, Nairobi

Economy: Agriculture is an important part of the Kenyan economy. Kenyans grow many crops, including corn, bananas, wheat, and sugarcane. Major exports include tea and coffee. About half of all Kenyan workers are employed in service industries, which include selling goods in stores, tourism, banking, insurance, education, health care, and government work. Industry plays a small part in the Kenyan economy. The major manufactured goods are processed foods and beverages. Soda ash, fluorspar, and rubies are mined in Kenya, and oil has recently been discovered there.

Currency: The Kenyan shilling. In 2014, 88 Kenyan shillings equaled US$1.

System of weights and measures: Metric system

Literacy rate: 87%

Currency

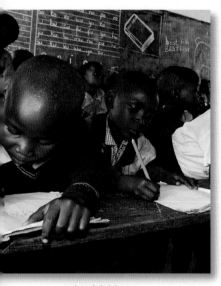

Schoolchildren

Jomo Kenyatta

**Common Swahili
words and phrases:**

jambo	hello
kwaheri	good-bye
tafadhali	please
asante	thank you
ndiyo	yes
hapana	no
harambee	let's work together
rafiki	friend
uhuru	peace

Prominent Kenyans:

Julie Gichuru (1974–)
TV newscaster

Jomo Kenyatta (ca. 1893–1978)
First president of Kenya

Richard Leakey (1944–)
Scientist and government official

Wangari Maathai (1940–2011)
Environmentalist and politician

Lupita Nyong'o (1983–)
Actor

Margaret Ogola (1958–2011)
Novelist and doctor

Ngugi wa Thiong'o (1938–)
Writer

Harry Thuku (1895–1970)
Political activist

To Find Out More

Books

▶ Burgess, Maryellen. *Life in Kenya.* New York: Rosen Classroom, 2013.

▶ Chambers, Catherine. *Swahili.* Chicago: Heinemann Library, 2012.

▶ Lock, Deborah. *The Great Migration.* New York: DK Publishing, 2012.

▶ Maathai, Wangari. *Unbowed: A Memoir.* New York: Anchor Books, 2007.

▶ Marcovitz, Hal. *Islam in Africa.* Philadelphia: Mason Crest, 2014.

▶ Nardo, Don. *The European Colonization of Africa.* Greensboro, NC: Morgan Reynolds, 2011.

Music

▶ *Kenya Special: Selected East African Recordings from the 1970s and '80s.* London: Soundway, 2013.

▶ *The Rough Guide to the Music of Kenya and Tanzania.* London: World Music Network, 2004.

▶ Visit this Scholastic Web site for more information on Kenya:
www.factsfornow.scholastic.com
Enter the keyword **Kenya**

Index

Page numbers in *italics* indicate illustrations.

tilapia, 78, 79
tortoises, 31
tourism, 13, *13*, 16, 23, 25, 82, 105
towns. *See* Lamu; Malindi.
transportation, 12, 23, *23*, 28, 43, *43*, 52, *53*, 74, 75, *75*, 84, 121, 122, *122*, 127
tree frogs, 31
tropical rain forests, 20, *20*, 34
Tsavo National Park, 37
tuk tuks (taxis), 23, *23*, 121
turtles, 31

U
ugali (food), 124, *124*, 125
Uganda, 15, 20, 22, 52, 78, 80, 81, 85
unemployment rate, 85
United States, 62, *62*, 78
University of Nairobi, 95

V
villages
  Mijikenda people, 99
  Takaungu, 102
volcanoes, 17, *21*
vultures, 34

W
Wasike, Godfrey Shiundu, 103
water, 13, *17*, 22, 72, 75, 90, 91, 92, 119
waterfalls, 18, *18*, 20
western plateau, 20
white-bellied go-away birds, 34
wildebeests, 27, 36, 37
wildflowers, 36
wildlife. *See* amphibian life; animal life; insect life; marine life; plant life; reptilian life.
women. *See also* people.
  agriculture and, 117
  as business owners, 81, 117

clothing, 100, 121, 123, *123*
dancing, *42*
education and, 120, *120*
employment, 81, 117, 120, *120*
foreign trade and, 43
government and, 67, *67*, 69
jewelry, 106, *106*
Kikuyu people, *42*
Lake Victoria region, *32*
Lake Turkana region, *17*
literature and, 112
Maasai people, 106, *106*
motherhood, 118–119, *118*
music and, 110
solar power and, 81
sports and, 115
water and, *17*, 119
World Heritage Sites, 99
World War I, 56, 91
World War II, 56

Y
Young Kikuyu Association, 55, 57

Z
Zanzibar, 48, 49, 50, 102, 123
zebras, 37

Meet the Author

MICHAEL BURGAN HAS WRITTEN MORE THAN 250 books for children and teens, most them about history or geography. This is his fourth book in the Enchantment of the World series. Previously, he wrote about Belgium, Chile, and the United States. He has also written many biographies. Some of his favorites include books on Hillary Clinton, Thomas Edison, and Nikola Tesla.

In writing this book, Burgan consulted many books, government Web sites, and Web sites of Kenyan newspapers. He also relied on the experiences of a friend, Mary Bowman-Kruhm, who has spent extensive time in Kenya and worked on a project to bring clean water to Maasai villages. She provided details of daily life that no book or Web site was likely to have.

Burgan majored in history at the University of Connecticut. In addition to writing books, Burgan also edits the newsletter for the Biographers International Organization (BIO). In his free time, he enjoys writing plays, traveling, and taking pictures. He lives in Santa Fe, New Mexico, with his cat, Callie.

Photo Credits

Photographs ©:

cover: Steve Bloom Images/Superstock, Inc.; back cover: John Warburton Lee/AWL Images; 2: Eric L. Wheater/Getty Images; 5: Jamen Percy/Shutterstock, Inc.; 6 center: Nordic Photos/Superstock, Inc.; 6 right: adrian arbib/Alamy Images; 6 left: Meng Chenguang/Xinhua Press/Corbis Images; 7 left: Friedrich Stark/Alamy Images; 7 right: Sean Sprague/age fotostock/Superstock, Inc.; 8: Tom Cockrem/Getty Images; 11: Kenneth Garrett/National Geographic Creative; 12: John Warburton Lee/Superstock, Inc.; 13: Nordic Photos/Superstock, Inc.; 14: Radius Images/Getty Images; 16: Nigel Pavitt/Getty Images; 17: John Warburton Lee/Superstock, Inc.; 18: Nigel Pavitt/John Warburton Lee/Superstock, Inc.; 19: John Warburton Lee/Superstock, Inc.; 20: Jake Lyell/Alamy Images; 21: Athol Pictures/Alamy Images; 22: Michael Nichols/National Geographic Creative; 23 top: Ariadne Van Zandbergen/Alamy Images; 23 bottom: Tom Cockrem/age fotostock/Superstock, Inc.; 24: Minden Pictures/Superstock, Inc.; 26 left: Tui De Roy/Minden Pictures; 26 right: Minden Pictures/Superstock, Inc.; 27: Gerard Lacz Images/Superstock, Inc.; 28: Stuart G Porter/Shutterstock, Inc.; 29: Robin Moore/National Geographic Creative; 30: Ryszard Laskowski/Dreamstime; 31: Mc Donald Wildlife Ph/Animals Animals/age fotostock; 32: Friedrich Stark/Alamy Images; 33: Papilio/Alamy Images; 34: Anna Omelchenko/Dreamstime; 35: Bob Smith/National Geographic Creative; 36: Minden Pictures/Superstock, Inc.; 37: Juergen Ritterbach/Alamy Images; 38: Xu Suhui/Xinhua/Landov; 40: Topham/The Image Works; 41: AFP/Getty Images; 42: Ariadne Van Zandbergen/Getty Images; 43: John Warburton Lee/Superstock, Inc.; 45: Severino Baraldi/Getty Images; 46: DeAgostini/Superstock, Inc.; 47: Angus McComiskey/Alamy Images; 49: Apic/Getty Images; 50: INTERFOTO/Alamy Images; 51: Mary Evans Picture Library/Alamy Images; 54: , NYC; 55: Corbis Images/Corbis Images; 56: SSPL/Planet News Archive/The Image Works; 57: TopFoto/The Image Works; 58: Press Association/The Image Works; 59: PA/TopFoto/The Image Works; 60: Baileys African History Archive/African Pictures/The Image Works; 61: PA Photos/Landov; 62: Stringer/Getty Images; 63: Tony Kurumba/Getty Images; 64: Felix Masi/African Pictures/The Image Works; 66: Photoshot/TopFoto/The Image Works; 67: AFP/Getty Images; 69: Thomas Mukoya/Reuters; 70: Nation Media/Getty Images; 72: Julinzy/Shutterstock, Inc.; 73: Thomas Mukoya/Reuters/Landov; 74 bottom: John Warburton Lee Photography/Alamy Images; 74 top: Ariadne Van Zandbergen/Alamy Images; 75: Antony Njuguna/Reuters/Landov; 76: Ton Koene/age fotostock/Superstock, Inc.; 78: Dereje Belachew/Alamy Images; 79: Robert Harding Picture Library/Superstock, Inc.; 80: Njuwa Maina/Reuters; 81 top: Robert Harding Picture Library/Superstock, Inc.; 81 bottom: Tony Kurumba/Getty Images; 83: Simon Maina/Getty Images; 84 top: Michael Smith/Dreamstime; 84 bottom: Ding Haitao/Xinhua Press/Corbis Images; 85: Benedicte Desrus/Alamy Images; 86: Sean Sprague/age fotostock/Superstock, Inc.; 88: Oleg Znamenskiy/Dreamstime; 89 top: Ariadne Van Zandbergen/Alamy Images; 89 bottom: AF archive/Alamy Images; 91: Sean Sprague/The Image Works; 93 top: Images of Africa Photobank/Alamy Images; 93 bottom: adrian arbib/Alamy Images; 94: Eye Ubiquitous/Newscom; 95 : Kenya Sights/Isaac Miriri; 96: Goran Tomasevic/Reuters; 98: Yann Arthus-Bertrand/Corbis Images; 99, 100: Meng Chenguang/Xinhua Press/Landov; 101: John Warburton Lee/Superstock, Inc.; 103: SAMUEL KISIKA/Demotix/Corbis Images; 104: Niels Busch/Getty Images; 106: Piers Cavendish/Impact/HIP/The Image Works; 107: Ariadne Van Zandbergen/Alamy Images; 108: Eric L. Wheater/Getty Images; 109: David Mbiyu/Demotix/Corbis Images; 110: Tony Kurumba/Getty Images; 111: Isaac Arjonilla/Zuma Press; 112: Jaguar PS/Shutterstock, Inc.; 113: David Mbiyu/Demotix/Corbis Images; 114: Julius Mwelu/Twenty Ten/Africa Media Online/The Image Works; 115: Boris Streubel/Getty Images; 116: Danita Delimont/Getty Images; 118 top: Tom Cockrem/age fotostock/Superstock, Inc.; 119: Papa Bravo/Shutterstock, Inc.; 120: Agencja Fotograficzna Caro/Alamy Images; 121: Jirisykora83/Dreamstime; 122 top: Ric Francis/Zuma Press; 122 bottom: dbimages/Alamy Images; 123: Tina Manley/Alamy Images; 124: Ariadne Van Zandbergen/Alamy Images; 125: Harrison Smith/Getty Images; 126: epa european pressphoto agency b.v./Alamy Images; 127 : Kenya Sights/Isaac Miriri; 130: Tom Cockrem/age fotostock/Superstock, Inc.; 131 top: Julinzy/Shutterstock, Inc.; 131 bottom: Nigel Pavitt/John Warburton Lee/Superstock, Inc.; 132 top: Athol Pictures/Alamy Images; 132 bottom: Michael Smith/Dreamstime; 133 top: Kenya Sights/Isaac Miriri; 133 bottom: PA/TopFoto/The Image Works.

Maps by XNR Productions, Inc.